Everest Canada

Everest

Canada
The Ultimate Challenge

AL BURGESS AND JIM PALMER

Foreword by The Rt. Hon. Roland Michener, P.C. Q.C.
Patron, Canadian Mount Everest Society

Stoddart/Toronto
A member of the General Publishing Group

First published in 1983 by

Stoddart

A Division of General Publishing Co. Limited
30 Lesmill Road
Toronto, Ontario

Published simultaneously in the United States by

Beaufort Books

and in the United Kingdom by

Hodder & Stoughton Limited

Canadian Cataloguing in Publication Data

Burgess, Alan.
    Everest Canada: the ultimate challenge

ISBN 0-7737-2009-X

*1. Mountaineering — Everest, Mount.   2. Mountaineers —
Canada — Biography.   3. Everest, Mount — Description.
I. Palmer, James.   II. Title.*

GV199.44.E85B87   796.5'22'095496   C83-098589-1

Painting of Mount Everest (pp. 120–121) reproduced by
permission of the artist, Murray Hay. Special thanks are also
extended to Equinox, The Magazine of Canadian Discovery.

Typesetting by DSR Typesetting Limited
Colour separations by Herzig Somerville Limited
Printed and bound by Bryant Press Limited

FRONT COVER PHOTOGRAPH: Tim Auger
DESIGN: Brant Cowie/Artplus Ltd.

Printed and bound in Canada

CONTENTS

FOREWORD

The Canadian mountaineers and their supporting Sherpas, whose dramatic climb to the top of Mount Everest in October 1982 raised so much interest in Canada and abroad, have now told the story in their own words.

Notwithstanding the odds against success and even survival, such an adventure had, for more than 60 years, been the goal of other expeditions, large and small. Some climbed for national or personal glory, some for the sport of it. However, Canadian Alpinists, good as they were, had previously been content, with a few individual exceptions, to accept the challenge of their own Rocky Mountains or other accessible peaks.

When a Canadian Mount Everest expedition was finally put together (and registered as the Canadian Mount Everest Society), it was financially sponsored by Air Canada and other contributors, and it was elaborately equipped and organized, both for the climb and for instant reporting by satellite from the climbers to the media.

Consequently the Canadian public watched with admiration and high hopes the preparation and departure of the team, and its establishment in the Base Camp on remote Mount Everest itself. But the public had little preparation for the almost immediate disaster the team experienced as it began to move supplies towards the upper camps. Loss of life is always a risk in a such climb, but certainly no one on the ground or at home anticipated that a terrific avalanche, followed by ice falls, and glacial movement in the Khumbu Valley, would take four lives in three days, before serious climbing had even begun. And the Khumbu Valley, which had to be traversed with these supplies, was no place to loiter.

Such misfortune was shattering to both climbers and Sherpas. In the aftermath, the Canadian team split, with some members leaving the expedition. The reduced team of climbers, in haste to achieve and justify the whole program, spent no time in bringing up further supplies, or perfecting their communications. They pushed with all speed for the top. Twin summit attempts were launched in the early hours of October 5 and 7.

Canadian reaction, which had earlier been muted by the deaths, the defections, and less-than-perfect reporting, was now enthusiastic. Congratulations were immediate and generous. The homecoming team is still being acclaimed as they move about the country.

This authentic book will confirm not only the courage and skill of the men themselves, but their success against difficulties as a great episode in the history of Canadian mountaineering.

Roland Michener

The Rt. Hon. Roland Michener, P.C. Q.C.

PREFACE

The Alpine Club of Canada first had formal contact with the Everest Expedition when Roger Marshall applied several years ago on behalf of a small group from Golden, B.C., for endorsement for Everest by the South Col in 1982. Shortly after the endorsement was granted, the leadership was transferred to George Kinnear of Calgary, and the expedition developed under him into a large and elaborate expedition to an unclimbed route on the South Pillar. Unfortunately, in the last months before the expedition, he suffered from a detached retina, and had to step down in favor of the third leader Bill March. It was Bill who led the expedition to its successful ascent by the South Col. It seems that the expedition had the right three leaders in the order it needed them—Marshall with the courage to start it, Kinnear with the determination to organize it thoroughly, and March to lead it in the field.

Its success, of course, is due to the skill, determination, and courage of the whole team, which includes the high altitude Sherpas who played such an essential role. But its success could not have occurred without the generous help of the expedition's principal sponsor, Air Canada, and its representative Mike Breckon, and of the many other organizations that contributed so much in so many ways, as described in detail in the appendices to this book. The work of the Mount Everest Society and its officers was crucial in raising this support.

The tragedies in the Khumbu Icefall, in which first an avalanche from high on the west face of Everest and then a collapse in the icefall killed four people, almost destroyed the expedition. It is easy to say that four deaths are about average for an expedition of this size to a very high mountain, and that is true: an average of about one in ten die in serious attempts on the world's highest mountains. But that does nothing to lessen the tragedy. Whether we should encourage expeditions like this where the most probable result is one in ten dead is a problem that has no simple answer.

The tragedies and their aftereffects are described in greater detail than is usual in mountaineering books, and there are many quotations from diaries written at the time. This may be for many the most interesting part of the book. We all like to learn how men have dealt with major tragedies, partly from voyeurism, but perhaps mostly because we may learn how better to face our own. The men who finally reached the decisions—some to go and some to stay—are real men with real strengths and real weaknesses, and the route to the decisions was not always as straight as we should like, after the event, such things to have been. But they rarely are. What is striking is how a group of men, after two major tragedies, reached very clear and very dignified and very creditable decisions by quite torturous paths. The book is well worth the price for this part alone. The account of the climb, which has plenty of its own fascination, is pure bonus. I strongly recommend the book to anyone interested in mountain climbing or the behavior of men under stress.

Ted Whalley,
President, Alpine Club of
Canada

PRELUDE

A JAGGED CRACK formed 3,000 feet up the face of the Everest West shoulder, half a mile across and 20 feet deep in the compacted, permanent snow. Then it came off, a wall 3,000 feet high, sliding down as one slice.

Early morning light. Tim's eyes met mine. We watched each other, waiting. The skin of the tent began to quiver. The strange rushing sound intensified, began coming from everywhere, became a roar. The poles stuttered and whined, the air filled with ice mist, the nylon exploded with air blast. Tim's eyes widened, mirroring my own racing fears.

A white wall as high and wide as he could see stormed out of the sky. He shouted but could not hear his voice. It threw him somewhere, into pain, where he could see nothing, where he couldn't breathe.

"Roger, Pat, we copy. Report positions, over! Report positions of personnel, over!"

Its edge accelerated over the gullies and buttresses, sometimes soaring into the night sky, sometimes gouging, blasting out tons, breaking into blocks like rolling houses, the snow and even the air rushing, thousands and thousands of tons, faster and faster.

They moved by the flickering light of their headlamps through a gallery of glittering shapes and deep shadows, over the seracs, the smooth bulges and cornices of crevasse edges. Here and there crystal snowflakes floated through the beams of light. Sometimes they heard a rumble, far away.

The massive ice towers that loomed around the tiny human figures were nothing in its path. They exploded like splintery wood, jagged pieces ploughed into the maelstrom, silvery white, churning, hissing in fury like giant serpents, plunging down on the puny paths of men.

Horrible silence . . . smothering pressure . . . an immovable mass. The jumar is jammed, the rope stretched. . . . The snow is everywhere on his body, packed against his bare skin, numbing him. His muscles struggle to shiver against the pressure. The snow in his throat stays there. He can't get it out. Can't do anything.

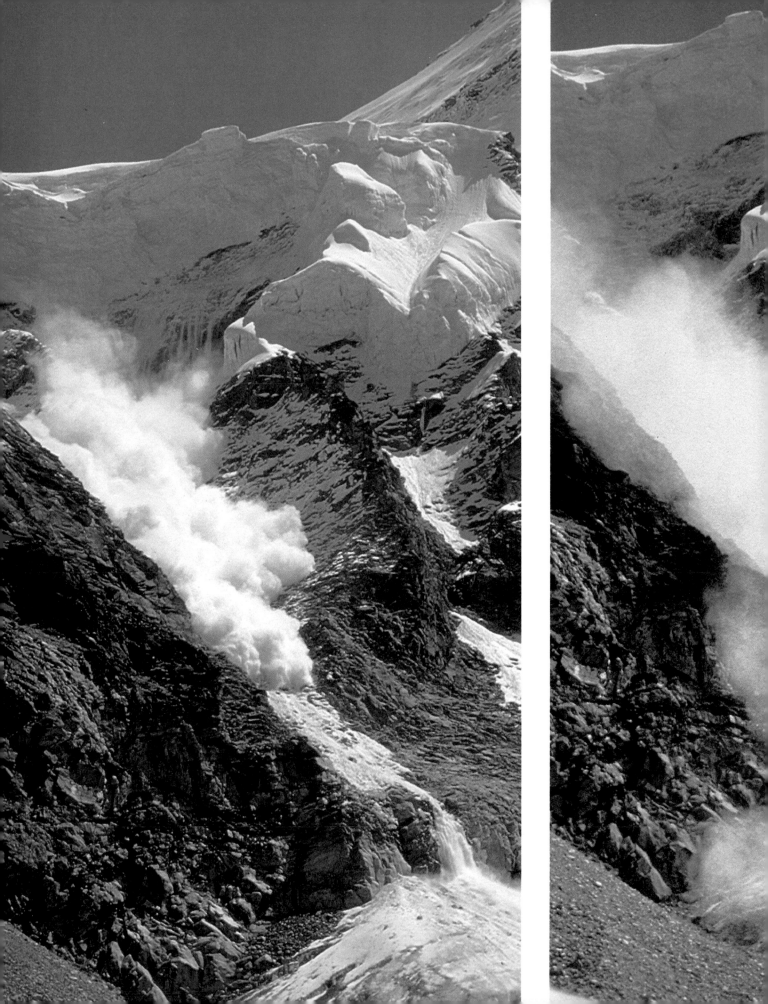

In a heavy snowfall, the sky overcast, I descended to Base Camp, a drab compound of snow-laden canvas, grey stone, and frozen boxes.

A lone figure stood quietly by the rough stone altar, the prayer flags flapping gently, the wisps of sweet smoke spiralling upward.

As I took the last few steps, I could sense the fear and doubt in the unfocussed stares and remote, hollow voices of those who greeted me.

This book is dedicated to the four men who lost their lives on the
Canadian Mount Everest Expedition.

Blair Griffiths, *cameraman*
Ang Tsultim, *high altitude Sherpa Khumjung*
Dawa Dorje, *high altitude Sherpa Thame*
Pasang Sona, *high altitude Sherpa Kunde*

TRUE TO STYLE

MOUNTAINEERING'S occasional association with world exploration or national prestige ("planting the summit flag") has resulted in the popular belief that the whole point is simply to "get to the top." This is sometimes true (in the sense that the point of golf is to put a ball in a cup), but the definition somehow misses the complex of traditions, conventions, ideals, and ethics that climbers generally call "style," in which lies their fascination with the sport.

Everest and its nearby Himalayan sisters have lured generations of mountaineering's finest, and are therefore a showcase for the ever-changing concept of "style."

From the beginning, Everest was a classical, mythical heroine. She was discovered from a distance by the Grand Survey of India in 1852 to be the highest mountain in the world. Once she was seen, it was her fate to suffer the human compulsion to find a way close to her, to touch her, then, by almost any means, to touch her summit. A casual period followed, during which other relatively easy paths were explored, until that paled; then the determination arose to probe her deeper, find secrets, test oneself against her, dare her to resist; to find her strengths, her truest, most powerful qualities.

In this process, she was gradually handed from the explorer to the mountaineer. Even on the earliest expeditions, however, there was evidence of the conventions and ethics that play such a large role in today's sense of "style."

Between 1922 and 1938, six British expeditions attempted Everest by the North Ridge. Most of these expeditions were small, partly out of naivete and necessity, but also out of a sense that this was the reasonable, dignified way.

In 1938, H. W. Tilman reached a height of 27,750 feet (8 458 m) on the North Ridge with a group of seven people. In his view, "any number more than one constitutes a large party." He maintained that any expedition which couldn't be planned on the back of an old envelope was over-organized. He also wanted to dispense with radios, oxygen, and other superfluous equipment.

Oxygen had first been used (and its use criticized on ethical grounds) in 1922. When Norton reached a height of 28,100 feet without it, on the ill-fated Mallory expedition of 1924, purists intensified their questioning, not only of its ethical purity, but also of its necessity. Tilman conceded, however, that *should* they find themselves in fair weather and within striking distance of the summit, only to be defeated by lack of oxygen, they would look "uncommonly foolish." After the trip, though, he felt that rationale to have been "rather cowardly."

Tilman was by no means typical of his day, when most of his colleagues believed that the summit should be reached by any method· possible. He was speaking for a cult that would remain in hiding for many years, obscured by the momentum of the "large-scale" style.

The logistics of this large-scale approach boggle the mind. It can take 600 loads of equipment, moved on the backs of yaks and porters into Base Camp at the foot of the mountain, to sustain a two-month siege. Of these loads, 350 may be ferried to Camp I by low-altitude Sherpas. This enables perhaps 200 loads to be hauled by fewer, stronger Sherpas and climbers to Camp II. Fifty loads might reach Camp III, and only eight may be in place for the one-day summit push from Camp IV, with a selected minimum of equipment and manpower.

In 1950, a large, well-organized French expedition led by Maurice Herzog climbed Annapurna I, the first of the 8,000-metre (26,247 feet) mountains to be conquered. In 1953, the summit of Everest was reached by Edmund Hillary and Tenzing Norgay. This large, military-style expedition led by Sir John Hunt had taken the mountain by the South Col route, with 20 Sherpas, 10 climbers, and tons of equipment and supplies. The Germans tackled Nanga Parbat in a similar fashion.

The same year, the Americans tried to climb K2, the second-highest mountain in the world, with only eight climbers, a small number of Hunza porters, no oxygen, and only 125 pack loads of equipment. However, this relatively small expedition failed. This seemed to prove the point: to climb an 8,000-metre mountain you needed the personnel, the equipment, the technology, the depth, and staying power of the large expeditions.

The remaining 13 of the world's 8,000-metre mountains were soon climbed by their easiest routes, using the proven methods of 1953. Once this was done, however, it was time for the next stage, the scaling of their more difficult ridges and faces. This era opened in 1970, with the ascent of the daunting 10,000 foot South Face of Annapurna. The kinds of technical challenges offered by the face had been overcome before, but never for 10,000 vertical feet, and never up to an elevation of 26,000 feet.

Other Himalayan "big walls" then began to fall to modern methods. After a number of attempts, the difficult South West Face of Everest was taken in 1975. The Yugoslavs climbed the South Face of Makalu and then went on to climb one of the longest and most difficult routes in the Himalayas, the complete West Ridge of Everest, in 1979. The Japanese climbed the 10,000 foot (3000 m) ice couloir on the North Face of Everest in 1980. In the spring of 1982, the first Russian expedition to Nepal climbed an even more difficult route on the South West Face of Everest.

With each new conquest, the self-criticism intensified in the mountaineering community. There was a growing consensus that *homo equipmens* was getting out of hand, and that the spirit of mountaineering was being lost. It was time for a return to style, to challenge for the individual. In fact, in some quarters, this was already happening. On remote, sheer, snow-blasted, ice-crusted, wind-riven crags and fangs in Patagonia, Peru, Alaska, Pakistan, and the lower Nepalese Himalaya, small teams of minimally equipped climbers were pushing the "mountains of the mind" to ever loftier heights.

Although Canadian climbers are too modest to point it out, we all know that Canadian Earl Denman, alone and equipped with nothing but his ice axe, boots, and backpack reached just a tad below the North Col of Everest in 1947. Even though an exact term for his style has not yet been agreed upon in the climbing fraternity, other stylistic terms *are* gaining currency.

"Lightweight" refers to a style between the extremes of large, military-style operations and some of the almost completely unsupported solo or small ("alpine style") ascents currently being attempted. It aims to reduce the number of Sherpas and climbers while keeping the ambitious goals previously attained with more resources. Fixed ropes and camps may still be used, but the bulk of the work is done by the climbers themselves. In 1981, five Canadians climbed the North East Spur of Dhaulagiri in this style. This was the first Canadian expedition to climb an 8,000-metre mountain and the smallest team ever to attempt this route.

One of many conceivable refinements is to omit supplementary oxygen. The prophet of this advance is Reinhold Messner, who wrote:

> For my own part, I had not come to Everest because I had an
> ambition to climb it at any price. My desire was to get to know it,
> in all its magnitude, its difficulty, and harshness, and I was deter-

mined to foreswear the summit if I couldn't reach it unaided by breathing equipment. As I have said, modern oxygen apparatus has the effect of reducing the height of Everest to around 6,000 metres. If I want this experience I don't have to go to Everest at all. But if I do want to experience Everest's unique sheer bulk, then to be able to feel it, sense it, I have to climb without any technical tricks.

In 1978, although part of a larger expedition, he and Peter Habeler reached the summit of Everest without oxygen. Later that same year, Messner soloed the Diamir Face of Nanga Parbat in three days without oxygen.

In pure "alpine style", a climber reverts to the beautiful simplicity of the average weekend mountaineering buff, fills his rucksack with equipment and food, and sets off to reach the summit in one continuous push, through however many bivouacs or camps, sunsets, sunrises, storms, sandwiches, and wild times it takes. The difficulties of this style, as one can imagine, are greatly increased at elevations above 8,000 metres!

The first 8,000-metre mountain to be climbed by this pure style was Hidden Peak in Pakistan, by Messner and Habeler in 1975. Increasingly, the style is moving up from lower elevations to confront the world's great high-altitude challenges. As the great French alpinist Lionel Terray wrote in his *Conquistadors of the Useless,* "For those who sought to define their own nature in the combat of man against the mountain there would soon be no solution but the desperate ways of the solo climber and the winter mountaineer."

In 1980, Messner climbed the North Ridge of Everest in one single, continuous push, again solo and without oxygen.

Then, as though further to fulfill Terray's prediction, in 1980 the Nepalese government officially opened the new Winter Season. The previous year, a Polish expedition had climbed Everest on February 17 —17 days after the end of the official winter season. Although the climb was unrecognized by the Nepalese government, mountaineers recognized it sufficiently to try to outdo it. The 1980–1981 Winter Season saw a new wave of winter expeditions, most of which failed.

During that winter, my twin brother Adrian and I joined six other climbers on the British Everest West Ridge winter expedition. We did not use oxygen or high-altitude Sherpas. After two months of desperate struggle we reached a height of 24,000 feet and the end of our endurance. This was the most demanding climb I had ever been involved in, and we had to concede that, above 20,000 feet, winter conditions presented a new challenge indeed.

In the 1981–1982 Winter Season, a Canadian group that included my brother and me climbed Annapurna IV (24,688 feet), at that time the highest mountain to be climbed in winter. As we write in the winter of 1982–1983, Messner has just given up on Cho Oyu, the Japanese have given up on Manaslu, and are currently unheard from on Dhaulagiri. The great Japanese climber Kato reached Everest's summit, but he and a partner died on the descent. Also in the winter of 1982–1983, the French attempted the West Ridge of Everest, but were repulsed.

Even though nature is not creating new mountains every year, she is managing, aided by climbers' inventiveness, to create plenty of new challenges. These challenges, and therefore the prowess, and therefore the pride are all based upon style. The Canadians who went to climb Everest in 1982 encountered more than a mountain. We encountered a very complex tradition that tested our definitions of style and of self.

 ## STRANGERS IN A STRANGE LAND

NOTHING IS STRANGER in a strange land than the sight of something familiar. I think this paradox is the essence of culture shock. If only we could keep Everest locked in our minds the way Hillary's team photographed it, if only Kathmandu would remain the exotic mystery her name has traditionally evoked, we could handle it more easily. But today's traveller finds that modern economics has ripped much of Nepal from the middle ages and thrown parts of her headlong into the jet age, leaving bits of her scattered everywhere between.

Tourism is Nepal's main industry, and an important part of tourism is mountaineering. Every year, 70 or 80 expeditions come to Nepal to climb a list of 56 "expedition peaks." These range from massive national expeditions to the smallest alpine efforts. The new Ministry of Tourism (mountaineering section) has streamlined bureaucratic procedures for expeditions, which has resulted in more expeditionary climbing. In fact, many mountains are now designated as "trekking peaks" and can be climbed with much simpler permit procedures, and this no doubt has added hundreds of ascents per year.

There are now three very full seasons of mountaineering and trekking activity, all centered in Kathmandu, a new world alpine centre, where climbers from all over the world know each other, compare notes, hide or share competitive secrets, and recuperate between climbs.

Mountaineering is a major industry in Nepal, and Kathmandu has many Trekking equipment shops dealing in equipment sold at the end of major expeditions.

The thatched huts of a small settlement a few miles from Lamasangur, the traditional beginning point for the walk-in to Everest Base Camp.

The early section of the walk-in took the team through lush rice paddies watered by heavy monsoon rains.

A Himalayan expedition even a few years ago was considered a once-in-a-lifetime mountaineering experience. Now some climbers are going from one expedition directly to another, carrying the fitness and acclimatization of one right into the next. They are spending much longer at altitude than climbers used to, and thus can acclimatize much more quickly. For example, Reinhold Messner climbed Kangchenjunga in Nepal in the spring of 1982, went to Pakistan in the summer to climb two 8,000-metre mountains there, then returned to Nepal in the late fall for the Cho Oyu winter expedition. This was exceptional but it is becoming less so.

I went out from Canada in the late fall of 1980 to do the Everest West Ridge in winter, stayed in Nepal trekking during the late winter and spring, then climbed Dhaulagiri in April and May. I had only been back in Canada for a few months when I left in November 1981 for the Anna-purna IV winter expedition, and returned to Kathmandu in January to set up the next few months' trekking. I spent a lot of time through the spring at elevations above 10,000 feet. When summer came, I was climbing in Ladakh in Northern India, then returned to Nepal in late June, 1982 to take part in the Canadian Everest expedition. In the last three years I have been on six expeditions. This has had a positive effect on the way I perform at altitude, and the level of activity is typical of a new kind of Himalayan climber.

Such a climber favours lightweight expeditions. With few or no support porters or Sherpas, less red tape, and much reduced financial needs, the modern climber can dream of a winter climb in Nepal, linking up with a pre-monsoon climb in Nepal, followed by a trip to Northern India or Pakistan during the monsoon, and a return to Nepal during the post-monsoon period. The irony is, of course, that now that hordes of Westerners are arriving, much of the exotic remoteness they came for is evaporating.

Modern roads and bridges have cut many days of jungles, ridges, rivers, and valleys off the old walk into Everest Base Camp that used to begin in Kathmandu or even India. Pilatus Porter or Twin Otter STOL ("short take off and landing") aircraft fly regular routes out of Kathmandu to Pokhara, Lukla, Biratnager and many other moun-taineering or trekking points. One hotel maintains bottled oxygen in its bar and rooms.

The flights to Lukla bring Everest, Cho Oyu, Lhotse, and a number of other fine mountains to within a five-day walk. The new East-West highway has brought many previously remote expedition objectives within the range of the new lightweight style.

Trekking companies have been set up to act as agents for expeditions. High-altitude Sherpas, cooks and kitchen staff, and mail runners can be hired on the basis of complete résumés. Many of the Sherpas are far more experienced than some of the Western climbers. Two-thirds of the Sherpas on the Canadian expedition had previously climbed above 8,000 metres, some many times.

Of course, all this "progress" has caused cultural losses, and one hears laments—even from climbers—for the early fifties, "the golden age of 8,000-metre summits." However, I find Kathmandu fascinating, just the way it is today with its vivid visual interplay of modern and medieval. Stylized statues of Buddha and representations of Hindu gods in their intricate temples co-exist peacefully with modern urban bustle. I thoroughly enjoy the clean hotels, cheap restaurants, good food, and other big-city amenities. As a legacy from the sixties, Kathmandu has its own European-American area of hippy shops and coffee houses, called "Freak Street," each year less and less unconsciously doing its own thing for Nepalese tourism. I find it somehow comforting to see this manifestation of my own counter-cultural past gradually being co-opted by throngs of world travellers. It gives one a sense of progress.

Part of this commercial momentum derives from trekking. Nepal's passes and valleys are connected by hundreds of miles of medieval trading paths that are now open to the Westerner. One can pass weeks walking from Kathmandu to Everest, or circling the Annapurna Massif, or exploring many other routes that seem to unroll before you one fascinating scene after another. The Ministry of Tourism has deliberately developed trekking to attract tourism. Expedition climbers 10 years ago rarely encountered Westerners. Now they pass hundreds on the trails, especially en route to Everest Base Camp. These streams of imported languages, clothing, equipment, music (portable tape recorders), and money, penetrating into the old high regions, have had a very noticeable effect.

The Sherpas are an innovative, adaptive people, and they have wasted no time in capitalizing on the popularity of their country. Some of them have now organized their own trekking companies and run package trips for tourists. Pertemba, the first Sherpa to reach the summit of Everest twice, is now a businessman working in the tourist industry. Expedition equipment now finds its way via Sherpas to Tibetan- and Sherpa-owned trekking shops for rental or sale to tourists.

Sherpas are also becoming mountaineers in their own right, much as the Swiss did when their country was invaded by foreign mountaineers in the nineteenth century. In 1981–1982 Tilicho Peak (23,398 feet) was climbed in winter by a very small group of Sherpas. This was the first

James Blench and Lloyd
Gallagher plod through
wall-to-wall paddy fields
on their way to Korantichap.

Two climbers pause to
enjoy the view. Below lies
a Sherpa village in the
district of Solu.

The trail to Everest Base
Camp from Kathmandu.

all-Sherpa expedition and it was climbed in modern lightweight style. A joint Sherpa-American expedition has received its permit for 1983 to climb Everest from the North, traverse the mountain, and descend to Nepal via the South Col route. Expeditions organized by the Sherpas themselves will surely become more popular, especially if funding is available.

The majority of Sherpas climb for a livelihood, of course, but as a Sherpa adds summits, cols, and high camps to his résumé, his pay scale improves, and he is more likely to be appointed Sirdar (leader of the expedition Sherpas). So there is a harmony of objectives when a Sherpa husband and father decides to take in a summit here and there.

Everest is no longer the mountain Edmund Hillary climbed and Nepal is no longer the country Tenzing Norgay grew up in. I anticipated that by the time many members of the Canadian expedition got to the relative cultural isolation of Base Camp, they would already be somewhat changed in their expectations and perceptions from the individuals who stepped off the plane in Kathmandu.

CHORTEN FOR A FRIEND

ROGER MARSHALL and I entered the Kathmandu Valley in a Nepalese Airlines flight from Delhi. The green July lushness of central Nepal spread below us, while the barrier of the Himalayas stretched as far as we could see, toward Tibet. To the north and east of the flight path, we could see Everest and could pick out the dark rock of the South West Face.

Roger is a bearded, rough-hewn figure, a classical British Lake District rock climber whom I had known for years. In fact, it had been while bouncing along the gravel road toward the Phantom Crags of Alberta's Ghost River in 1978, on our way to do some rock climbing, that he had mentioned he thought his Everest permit might come through. He asked me if I was interested. I said yes, and we said no more about it.

As it turned out, he got the permit and was thus the first member of the Canadian Mount Everest Expedition. As it also turned out, I was the last one to be invited to join it. Now we were together, arriving in Kathmandu ahead of the expedition, and sharing the excited realization that the whole thing had actually come off.

As the plane sank into the valley, and the busy, earth-coloured geometry of the city rose up to meet us, I felt as though I were coming home. I had spent most of the previous nine months in Nepal and it had become almost as familiar as Canada. In the airport, the shouts, smells, heat, bustle, business suits, tribal garb, saris, turbans, bracelets, officials, porters, luggage boys, mixed languages, and dramatic gesticulations of eastern commerce all seemed welcoming after my summer in the Indian mountains.

I had last been here six weeks before with other Canadian Everest climbers, to get some of our equipment hauled high up into the Khumbu Everest area for storage. Most of the equipment had been flown from Kathmandu into Lukla, a little settlement at the entrance to the Everest Khumbu valley, and from there had been taken still higher by yaks and Sherpa porters to a Sherpa house at Kunde, above the Sherpa trading centre called Namche Bazaar.

Some of the equipment, however, such as propane and oxygen bottles, could not be flown, and had to go by surface from Kathmandu. ("Surface" means uncertain roads, footpaths and swinging bridges.) Climbers Dwayne Congdon and Jim Elzinga had supervised the first 80 loads of this gear, then returned home. The gear was carried on the willing backs of small but sinewy local porters. I accompanied the second crew of these sturdy men and women, to ensure that our propane bottles weren't traded somewhere up in the passes for Tibetan salt, Indian gold, or Chinese rifles. This left between 50 and 100 loads of gear that would have to be portered up when the main expedition arrived in August. At that time the roads and trails would be much more difficult in the monsoon rain.

During the pre-monsoon walk-in, I heard that there was an Austrian expedition on Cho Oyu, an 8,000-metre mountain near Everest. A climbing friend, Reinhard Karl, was on the team and Gokyo, a high village near our trail, was only three hours from the Austrian Base Camp. Once my porters had reached their destination, I took a side trail up into the Gokyo valley. Reinhard was on the mountain, but I visited his wife, Eva, and his sister, Ilona, near Base Camp. It was pleasant getting to know them and finding out how the climb was going.

One week later, back in Kathmandu, I heard that Reinhard had been killed by an ice avalanche. I then spent a draining week with Eva and Ilona, deeply involved in their loss and grief and also in the ugly administrative hassles associated with the death.

This experience had a powerful effect on me. I have lost many good friends in climbing accidents and grieved for them. Yet there was always an understanding that each of us had freely chosen the risks because we loved climbing. But Eva and Ilona's loss of Reinhard was not a climbing loss to some shared ideal. It was loss of love and commitment between people who had shared not just one passion, but everything in their lives. Reinhard's death gave me a deeper grasp of the responsibilities climbers

bear for the risks they take. I promised Eva that when I went up with the Canadian group I would go up into the Gokyo valley, under the face of Cho Oyu, and build a *chorten,* or stone memorial, for her husband.

Now, arriving early with Roger, I had the opportunity to do that. The rest of the expedition wouldn't join us for three weeks. The monsoon is not the safest season in the Himalayan foothills, with washouts, mud slides, swollen rivers, and missing bridges, but I thought that Roger and I together would be all right.

After a week of tourism and organizing for the expedition in Kathmandu we left the Sheraton Hotel in a Nissan patrol-wagon driven by Marshall Gysi, a Canadian working in Nepal. He had kindly offered us a ride as far as Lamosangu or, road permitting, even further. A young Sherpa porter accompanied us, because we had tinned food to supplement the usual rice and *daal* (lentil beans) on the trail. Trekkers usually lose weight, but we wanted to keep our strength up, carrying 40-pound packs and getting a reasonable amount of protein.

Lamosangu is 46 miles from Kathmandu on an old, Chinese-built road. From there a new, Swiss-built road winds up to Korantichap, then drops steeply into the Tamba Kosi valley and crosses a brand-new suspension bridge. Past the bridge, we found that the situation deteriorated quickly. The truck ground its way upward over mud and shifting stone. We got as far as Namdu, a small village about an hour's drive from the end of the Swiss road. One look at the winding, broken trail just visible through the hot afternoon mists above the village told us it was time to start walking.

With only light packs, lightweight boots, shorts, and T-shirts, we quickly gained height on small footpaths winding up through green paddy fields. The lowland Tamang people were already out in the calf-deep water of the terraced paddies. They were barelegged, their cotton pantaloons tucked up, their seedbags on shoulder slings or around their waists, doubled over so that their hands could work under the water. The planting was just beginning. Plodding, yoked water buffalo moved the wooden ploughs through the mud ahead of the planters.

The workers noticed us and smiled and shouted and waved. Some of the younger ones had an urban look about them, and I knew they had only come out from Kathmandu to help their farming families with the seeding. It would be welcome help, I'm sure, because the work is back-breaking and every seed counts. Here, when there is no rice, there is no food.

As we hiked, the clouds appeared lower, the mist denser, and the expected afternoon rain began. The trail became slippery as water coursed down it. The air was still just as hot, the mists just as thick, the clouds just as low as before the rain, but now everything seemed to be part of a grey-green steam: paddies, trail, sodden vegetation, dripping thatched roofs, and our own soaked packs, T-shirts, soggy feet, and streaming hair. There was nothing to do but press on. We kept up our pace, which we called "double days," to cut the time to Namche Bazaar from the usual eight or ten trekking days down to four or five.

On the first day, we reached just past the small village of Yarsa, at about 6,000 feet. That night I enjoyed being under a thatched roof, sitting on the dirt floor, watching the woodsmoke from the cooking fire spiralling toward the smoke hole. We drank milk tea and added *daal bhaat* (cooked white rice and lentils) to the tinned beef our young Sherpa supplied from our pantry pack.

The simplicity and reality of our surroundings allowed us to put things into perspective a bit. We both felt we needed this peaceful interlude, in view of what had happened so far, and what was likely ahead.

Since Roger's invitation years earlier, I had been on Himalayan expeditions most of the time and was thus out of touch with later developments. Roger, however, had been in the thick of it. Three months after receiving the permit, he had been replaced as leader by the remaining team members. Taking his place was George Kinnear, a stocky, red-bearded associate professor of physical education at the University of Calgary. The climbers felt Kinnear, a native-born Canadian, had the sort of establishment image that would be required to attract sponsors. (Roger was allowed to be deputy leader. I presume this was to console him so that he would allow the new team and leader to share his permit, which he did.)

An enthusiastic and unco-ordinated expedition then grew, with a board of directors, many additions and deletions of climbers, and a headlong rush into the sponsorship game. The expedition became the target of a barrage of proposals, and quickly developed its own red tape, internal politics, budget crises, leadership skirmishes, and so on.

In short, it went through the upheavals inevitable to any national, large-scale, high-talent endeavour, and all things considered, was just the sort of thing I felt privileged not to have been involved in. (Although my name was on various lists, I had not officially been invited to join the expedition.)

It happened that my brother Adrian and I had been included on one of the Everest "training climbs," a winter expedition on Annapurna IV. After success on that climb, I received a letter from Peter Hillary inviting Adrian and me to join a lightweight Lhotse expedition in the fall of 1982. I knew Peter, and I had done some fine climbing in the Alps with Paul Moores, one of the other members of the expedition. They looked like a great group, the route was tempting, and I respected their proposed lightweight style. The problem was, it was to take place exactly at the same time — even from the same Base Camp site — as the proposed Canadian Everest expedition.

A couple of weeks later, I got a telegram in Kathmandu (from Bill March, the *third* leader!) inviting me to join the Canadians, and then I was *really* in a quandary. Impulsively, I telexed my acceptance, and rationalized my choice afterward. I reasoned that, if I personally ended up on the summit, it would help me to finance some future lightweight expeditions I had in mind. If, on the other hand, the Canadian expedition disintegrated, I could still step next door and join my brother and the New Zealanders on Lhotse. (Loyalty is a sometimes subtle thing!) Finally, I had been living on *tsampa, daal bhaat,* and *chang* (Nepalese food and drink) for a long time. All the expeditions I had been on were lightweight—the biggest had been made up of just eight men. The Canadian trip had 21 Westerners, 35 Sherpas and 700 loads of food and equipment. I figured that *had* to include some steak, gravy, bacon, eggs and rye whiskey. (So there you have it. For the climber, in the end, it's idealism.)

It was pleasant to be walking in ahead of the main expedition. Since we slept in small tea shops (a night's room and board rarely more than a dollar per person), Roger and I were free to walk all day until dark without the hassle of porters, finding campsites, and setting up camp. In the morning there was no elaborate repacking: we simply threw a couple of items in our packs, and stepped out onto the trail in the relatively fresh, clear morning air. Somehow the night cleared away the pungent smells of animals, cooking, smoke, sewage, and paddy water, and instead we breathed in the natural perfumes of beautiful valleys in the early morning sunlight.

For me, the scenery was familiar. This was the fourth time I had travelled this way, and around every turn I recognized a house or a cluster of trees. I find a great deal of pleasure in the walk-ins, swinging along in long strides, horizon following horizon. The mind becomes clear and focussed, while the muscles tighten and tone up. This is an essential stage for climbers arriving fresh from the West. The conditioning is significant. The daily height gains and losses can add up to 10,000 feet, and it is said that to reach Everest Base Camp you climb the height of Everest twice.

We had our first view of the mountains of Gaurishanker on the second morning, as we crossed a high ridge. It is incredible how you become visually preoccupied with the villages and valleys, until, just casually, you glance up, and suddenly you see those unbelievably powerful, majestic and *big* mountains, as though for the very first time. The

*An open-air dinner at
Korantichap. The
afternoon monsoon rains
often forced this social
meal indoors.*

ground we had already covered would take the main expedition four or five days with their caravan of laden porters.

The highest point on the walk-in is the Lamjura Pass. From the small village of Kenja, we followed a winding path, step after step, 5,000 vertical feet, to an 11,500 foot high rhododendron–covered ridge. And there, suddenly, it opens, a magnificent view, the gateway to the Sherpa country.

Then we had to sacrifice our height gain yet again, going down and down, through thick forest to the village of Jumbese in the Solu Khumbu area. This is the main village in the region, and used to be one of the richest of all Sherpa villages. In the time of the powerful Rana families in Nepal, the nearby town of Okadunga was where the lowland tax collectors met the highland tribes and the local Sherpas became the tax collectors for the mountain regions. This income, together with that from their extremely fertile land, gave them a tradition of wealth. The image no longer really fits, but to some extent the native sons on expeditions are still identified with it—perhaps especially by those other Sherpas of the upper Khumbu area, at the very foot of Mount Everest who, in recent years, have gained wealth, through tourism, trekking and expeditions.

From Jumbese we traversed around a wooded hillside, to Ringmo, a village famous for its apple *rakshi,* a spirit made from cider.

As we got further into the mountain ranges the rain decreased, to late afternoon showers and the humidity eased. We crossed the final ridge at the Traksindho Pass before the 5,000 foot descent down to the Dudh Kosi ("Milk River"). Until recently, the trade route from the lowlands wound up the western side of the river on a steep, difficult trail. Now, however, a suspension bridge crosses this vast, thundering gorge, opening onto an easier new trail northward to Namche Bazaar, the largest town in the area.

We passed many strings of porters: dark-stained, little medieval wood carvings of people, the nation's truckers, with the country's livelihood on their backs in woven *doko* baskets weighing 65 to 150 pounds. Both men and women were barefoot, in loose cotton pants or shirts. They smiled as they passed, modest peasant eyes looking up from under the straining headbands. Their teeth were stained from the chewing tobacco and sugar cane they often gnaw as they push, step by step, up and down the trails, their splayed toes grasping hold after hold.

Sometimes we passed them squatting around a small fire, making their twice-daily meal of rice. It was these people who would in a few weeks be carrying our expedition gear into Namche Bazaar, for transfer to yaks and Sherpa porters.

As we approached Namche Bazaar, the signs of Sherpa life and culture replaced that of the lowland Tamangs and Rais. Thatched roofs and woven bamboo or adobe walls were supplanted by more sophisticated two-storey stone buildings with large-eaved roofs made of axe-hewn wooden shingles. The upstairs floor of such houses is usually used for the living and cooking quarters, while the lower floor is used for livestock and winter fodder, so that the body heat of yaks, water buffalo, or sheep can rise into the living quarters.

In a lowland hut, one sits on a hard mud floor, leaning against a mud wall, near a simple mud fireplace. Higher up though, the Sherpa kitchen has metal utensils, large brass and copper urns for storing water, and brightly polished kettles and cooking pots. Tibetan rugs are rolled out over cushions or a wooden bench when visitors arrive.

The clothing, too, shows a difference. The lightweight cotton skirts or baggy trousers that are practical and comfortable in the hot, humid lowlands are replaced by heavier, woven wool garments, and yak skin hats and jackets suited to higher elevations.

Sherpa footwear was originally made from yak skin and woven wool from Tibet. Now these are commonly replaced by Chinese canvas basketball shoes, often worn with blue jeans or track suits, ski jackets, sweaters, balaclavas and sunglasses—expedition gear that is quickly replacing the yak robes and wool blankets that have been used for centuries.

Up higher now, our diet improved. Potatoes (the staple) were supplemented by *tsampa* (roasted barley flour), eggs, and cheese and curd from the yaks and *zopkiyo,* a yak-bovine crossbreed. These foods were served with Indian tea with milk and sugar or salted Tibetan tea that had been mixed with rancid butter in a long leather tube called a *dongmu.* We also found, as usual, ample quantities of chang in the tea houses and inns. This is roughly like beer or wine, depending upon how it is made and what it is made of, and has casual as well as festive roles. A favorite beverage is rice chang fermented to its full alcoholic potential. Other forms are made from corn or tsampa. A guest might receive a glass of chang with a small touch of tsampa flour or yak butter on the edge of the glass. This is usually drunk with appropriate ceremony and must be filled and drained three times.

We arrived in Namche Bazaar five days after leaving Kathmandu. This bustling commercial hub of the Khumbu district hangs on the point of a high spear-headed plateau that pushes between two branches of the Dudh Kosi. The slope falls off sharply, giving the impression that the town teeters on the brink. Constant winds add to the feeling of insecurity in this barren, hostile environment. Namche Bazaar developed as a trade centre between the lowlands of the Indian plains and the highlands of Tibet, an outpost at the limits of each culture.

Each Saturday there is an outdoor market where people from the lowlands come to sell such things as rice, eggs, tangerines, grains, peanuts, corn, butter, sugar, ginger, black tea, and chilis. This modern trade caters to local needs, but in winter, when the Sherpa people have little work to do and the weather is better for travelling, many will follow traditional urges, and in large groups with as many as 400 yaks, will take coloured Indian cottons, umbrellas, yak skins and meat, rice, and various Western goods over the Nampa La pass into Tibet.

In semi-legal trading houses on the Tibetan plateau, they exchange their goods for Tibetan wool, turquoise, musk oils, coral, and Tibetan artifacts for the tourists. The original trade in rock salt from Tibet is now dying, and the modern highway past Lamosangu through Barabise into Tibet has made the old trading route redundant. But the Sherpas continue to go over the Nampa La, as much for adventure as for profit.

Just a glance around Namche Bazaar had told us we were probably the only Westerners in town. We climbed the stone stairway to Lhakpa Dorje's trekking lodge, the Trekkers' Inn, and were welcomed in. We were warmly greeted, even though it was much too early for the tourist season and even early for expeditions. After settling in, we relaxed with tea and chang, in view of green hillsides covered in flowers, tin roofs reflecting afternoon sunshine, and, across the valley and upwards, the harsh, icy slopes of Tramserku.

After a day's rest and visiting with Lhakpa Dorje, we packed a few warm clothes for the higher elevations and left on the two-day hike to the lower slopes of Cho Oyu.

While the grass is green in the higher pastures during the monsoon season, many of the villagers move up and live in small wooden huts, tending their yaks. As we climbed higher, we realized that the festival of Yar Chang was in progress. Village families were carrying curd, rice, and chang into the upper pasture lands for two days of celebration and thanks to the gods for the health and increase of the yak herds.

During this festival, we reached the little collection of yak huts at 16,000 feet (4 900 m) called Gokyo. Here we intended to build Reinhard's chorten. The wind was howling down the valley, and the sky was overcast, with rain blowing over the lake. We banged on the thick wooden door of one of the huts and were immediately taken into the centre of the celebration and invited to sit by the fire next to the head of the family. The 50-year-old Nima Tenzing from Khumjung and I immediately recognized each other. What followed was a monstrous drunk.

25

A Sherpa elder in the Khumbu—within Sherpa society, the older people are treated with respect and consideration.

Namche Bazaar, the commercial and administrative centre of the Khumbu region, framed by tattered prayer flags. In recent years the old trade with Tibet to the north has begun to revive and some Sherpas are allowed across the border to trade.

Sherpa mother and child in Namche Bazaar, the capital of the Khumbu. Family ties are very strong in Sherpa society and children are given a great deal of love and affection.

For the next few nights we were guests; while we constructed the chorten, we were fed and kept well entertained.

The area surrounding the yak huts and Gokyo Lake is lush green pasture land, with tall yellow flowers scattered about on a carpet of small red and blue ones. It is one of the prettiest places in the Himalayas, and, with the awesome backdrop of Cho Oyu, it was a perfect memorial site for Reinhard Karl, the first German to climb Everest.

We found a small ridge overlooking the lake towards the South Face of Cho Oyu and built our monument. I carved Reinhard's name and the date of his death on a softer rock and we built it into the chorten. We covered the monument with the local flowers and I took photographs to send back to his wife.

I WOULD RATHER BE A RAVEN

OUR MISSION ACCOMPLISHED, we climbed nearby Gokyo Peak and looked out onto our mountain, Everest. The monsoon cloud was still blowing from the south and after a few glimpses of the summit we turned back to descend to Namche Bazaar. I knew that the tranquility of the off-season high pastures would contrast starkly with the intricate politics and complex logistics of a national mountaineering expedition. We would be meeting the rest of the expedition members in Namche Bazaar in a day or two. They would have left Kathmandu around July 26, and would take about 14 days to Namche Bazaar.

In addition to providing acclimatization and conditioning, I knew that Bill March, the new leader, had high hopes that the walk-in would give team members time to get to know each other, feel more comfortable doing things together, and shake out some of the divisions the group had inherited. Bill also hoped, I knew, to let some of his leadership style filter down through the group.

I sympathized with Bill's hopes. Yet I also knew that most Himalayan expeditions which have been successful, both in terms of objectives and morale, have been built around a strong leader who hand picked a team of climbers. These would be individuals who, first, could get along with him and, second, could get along with each other. Bill knew that, as the third leader of a very haphazardly selected team, he faced some tricky "fine tuning." He was asked after the climb, "If you had to do it all over again, what would you do differently?" He answered, without hesitation, "I would select my own team."

I had heard the "walk-in shake-down" concept cited on many other Himalayan expeditions, but I felt that it rarely produced the hoped-for results. Unfortunately, the kind of situation that *does* bind diverse elements is the stress of dealing with problems on the mountain. Inevitably, the team that comes down is tighter than the one that goes up.

A passage in Gordon "Speedy" Smith's diary, which I read later, makes it clear that conditions on the walk-in were less than idyllic:

> . . . the heavens opened up and we had a torrential downpour for two hours. Everything got soaked. I have never seen such a heavy downpour. The rain came straight through umbrellas and through the rucksacks and two plastic bags. We put the tents up in all this and absolute chaos reigned. Groundsheets were swimming in water and the tents were wet through. Surface water was pouring all over the campsite and all the packs were lying in puddles and covered with mud. I spent some time clutching my useless umbrella, still soaked from my bath. I couldn't even get my dry clothes on. Eventually I abandoned all hope and after five minutes of frenzied activity, got a tent up and climbed inside it. The mattresses were soaked but at least it was drier in the tent. Eventually the rain stopped. Everybody began salvage operations, but the weather was still too humid to dry anything.

Just the sort of thing to pull a team together!

Bloodsucking leeches provided another unpleasant diversion. They crawl up onto blades of grass and hang there, swaying, waiting for the passing feet of some warm-blooded creature. Others drop off from overhanging bushes and trees. At the end of each day it was a standard procedure to remove the accumulated leeches with salt water or the touch of a burning cigarette.

In fact, most diary entries were positive, mentioning brilliant visual effects, the vivid green of the mountain lowlands, hillsides covered in flowers, birds singing, and rhododendron bushes exuding their heady incense. The twisted overhanging rhododendrons imparted an aura of fairy-tale woodlands, and one climber recalled that Tolkien borrowed impressions from the Nepalese forests in the creation of his "Misty Wood." Such thoughts were perhaps a counterbalance to the aching muscles, sodden feet, various forms of dysentry, and implanted leeches that formed a questionable part of the team's conditioning for the world of rock and ice ahead of them.

Base Camp Manager Peter Spear and climber Dave McNab, like Roger and me, were travelling light and fast ahead of the main group.

A Tamang porter drinks a glass of tea heavily laced with milk and sugar.

The village of Kunde with chorten and mani stones. The hospital at Kunde, which serves the Khumbu region, is currently staffed by two Canadian doctors, Penny Darwin and Jaimie Ulrig, who provided medical assistance to the two Sherpas injured on the expedition.

Lloyd Gallagher, deputy leader, receiving a blessing from the head lama at the Tengboche monastery. On the left, climber Tim Auger awaits his turn in this traditional ceremony.

The immense south face of Nuptse rises above the acclimatization camp at Lobuche below the Khumbu glacier. In the foreground, yaks, the traditional beast of burden, graze on the alpine pasture.

They needed a few days' lead time to plan the siting and construction of the small town that would be our home for the next two months. On the evening of July 29, Peter and Dave arrived in Namche Bazaar. Roger and I had learned by grapevine that more Sahibs had arrived and rushed around to their lodge for our first contact with the army of Canadians.

The four of us spent a conversational but somehow slightly formal evening. My feeling of unease was intensified the next morning when Peter Spear took me to one side and handed me a letter. He stood waiting while I read it. It was from Bill March. I was astounded to realize it was in fact Roger's notice of dismissal from the team, ordering him to stay in Namche Bazaar until Bill caught up. The reason cited was a "breach of climber's contract."

I couldn't believe what I had read. What "breach"? Why now, so late, when the whole team was already on the way? I looked at Peter incredulously.

He filled me in on the team's meeting and discussions in Kathmandu, at which Bill had explained that rumours were circulating in Calgary about activities connected with Roger that could harm the expedition's image and, in turn, that of the expedition's sponsors. (Upon the expedition's return to Canada, the allegations against Roger were dropped as unsubstantiated, and the Canadian Mount Everest Society expressed its regret.) March had therefore decided to drop Roger from the team, and asked for a vote of confidence. Peter said the vote had been unanimous.

This tied in with other meetings I had known about over the past two years. Roger and I both knew that almost any excuse would do to get him off the team. We had thought, however, that by this time the danger had passed and he had survived. Roger is a good friend and, in my view, a very competent climber, given on occasion to abrupt, abrasive outspokenness. This quality endears him to some climbers, but can create tensions in a larger group like the Canadian Everest expedition. Yet, although Roger is headstrong, I had found that he never shirked his share of the work. On the Annapurna IV winter expedition the previous winter, he had been a tight-knit member of the team.

I dreaded the effect of this letter on Roger. He, after all, was the one who had got permission from the Nepalese government for the Canadian expedition in the first place, and he had been its missionary and its first leader. The complex manoeuverings that had resulted, four years later, in the present team with Bill as its leader had, however, generated undercurrents of distrust and enmity. Bill's fear, and that of the others, was that these tensions could resurface dangerously, high on the mountain.

The first sight of Everest from the upper Khumbu valley. The main summit on the left and the south summit on the right tower above the 25,850' high ramports of Nuptse. The final route taken followed just below the right skyline of the mountain.

The camp at Lobuche, last inhabited settlement before Base Camp. In the right foreground, patties of yak dung are dried on rocks to provide fuel for cooking and heating in a region where wood is scarce and costly.

Rusty Baillie expressed what he considered to be the team's consensus: "On any climbing expedition there are going to be times when you have to trust your partners with your life. If something comes up that causes you to doubt that trust, it's better to be wrong than sorry." Later, upon reflection, I found that I disagreed with Rusty's thinking. Most of the climbing team was untried, and by Rusty's logic I should have been reluctant to climb with any member of the expedition. Trust in climbing is built on climbing itself. I had climbed with Roger and found him to be a very strong and reliable partner. In many ways, when I was able to look back on the entire expedition and its outcome, I considered his dismissal to have been a severe loss to the venture.

Peter and I went to Roger, and I handed him the letter. He read it. He remained very quiet after completing it and I could tell that the shock was very deep.

Much later, Roger commented that he thought the basic reason underlying his dismissal was that he failed to fit the promotional mould that Bill March and John Amatt, the team's business manager, wanted of their climbers. In a sense, I felt this was true. I could hardly imagine Roger in his expedition uniform, clean-shaven, delivering a rehearsed "party line" to the media. The whole episode seems to me an indication that the expedition may have gotten out of proportion. If financial and public relations requirements result in fewer good climbers on the mountain, then something is wrong.

However, Tim Auger's diary records of the dismissal: "It was our first crisis, a testing and it really pulled us together. We started the walk-in with a feeling of solidarity that hadn't been there before."

Bill March arrived in the early afternoon of August 6. Roger and I were sitting with some Catalan climbers in a small trek shop, drinking tea and beer, when he burst in. He looked frustrated and obviously didn't want to cause a scene in front of the Catalans. Their concurrent West Ridge expedition would have its base camp only 200 yards from ours.

He asked to have a word with me and we walked outside. He explained his decision to me. He cited a clause in the climber's contract that protected the main sponsor, Air Canada, against embarrassment caused by any climber's actions, and said the rest of the team was unanimous in its decision to drop Roger. He added that he had already told the Nepalese Ministry of Tourism and the Canadian Consulate, so that his decision was now irreversible. He said he had done this deliberately so he couldn't be persuaded to change his mind. He asked for my reaction to the decision. I said I was sorry, and that I felt it would seriously weaken the team.

He kept looking at me. I said I would still climb. He nodded, with what I hoped was a little relief in his eyes, and turned to go back inside. Bill and Roger spent the rest of the evening drinking beer and talking.

The next day, August 7, the main group arrived. I could tell that it was coming when I saw the long lines of porters filing through Namche Bazaar, carrying brightly coloured boxes with the emblem of the Canadian expedition on them. Behind them came the throngs of Westerners and newly hired Sherpas in reds, blues, and yellows, shorts, T-shirts, baseball caps and rucksacks, headphones and cassette recorders and umbrellas. The tourist season had arrived with a bang. From now on the Khumbu valley would belong to expeditions and tourists, the peace and solitude gone until winter.

By evening Canadians were spread from the trekking lodges of Namche to the campground at Kunde, an hour's walk higher. I had dinner with the Kunde group that evening and later, drunk on chang and Canadian Club, I staggered back down in the thick mist and heavy rain to our lodge. Everyone seemed in high spirits. Just like tourists anywhere, they made insensitive demands in their own language and expected quick service from these already friendly and helpful people.

The next morning the Namche group left around mid-day to walk up to Kunde. Roger bid us all good-bye and with a look of total resignation disappeared down the valley.

We walked up the steep hillside for an hour, to the comfortably nestled villages of Kunde and Khumjung. That evening, in our long dining tent, we entertained the two Canadian doctors from Kunde Hospital. This hospital was built and financed by the Himalayan Trust, which was set up by Sir Edmund Hillary after his ascent of Everest in 1953. Hillary has done a great deal for this area, building schools and hospitals, and providing bridges and a constant water supply for the villagers.

It was my first night with the whole expedition and I was having trouble adapting to so many people, especially to noisy Westerners. But I realized that I would soon get over it. Now that Roger had left, there were 15 climbers, as well as three Base Camp personnel (Peter Spear, cook Kurt Fuhrich, and Dr. David Jones), Bruce Patterson, a journalist, and Blair Griffiths, a cameraman.

It helped to discover that Kurt Fuhrich was a jovial fellow whose company I could enjoy. He was outgoing and enthusiastic, unhindered by his heavily accented English. It turned out that he was a chef and restaurant owner in Banff, after some years as a cook for the 1972 Olympic Games, for a drilling camp 600 miles from the North Pole, and for the Shah of Iran. He had climbed in Borneo, and in Iran had scaled

Taboche, a minor peak near the village of Pheriche. In any other country this would be a major climb, but in the Khumbu it is dwarfed by the Everest massif.

Yaks making their way up the boulder-strewn Khumbu glacier. These hardy animals can carry twice the load of a porter and were used to bring supplies of fresh food to Base Camp.

39

Mt. Damavand (18,386 feet). I met Blair Griffiths, too, that evening. He was the 33-year-old cameraman working for Advertel who would be shooting film for the "production studio" being set up in Kathmandu.

On the morning of August 9, we struck camp and headed off on our first day's trek into the upper Khumbu area. As we descended from Khumjung I wandered along with Robert "Rusty" Baillie and Gordon "Speedy" Smith.

I have known Speedy for years. He is a warm, enthusiastic engineer with an undiluted Derbyshire drawl, who focusses intensely on whatever is at hand, whether it's a good laugh or some desperate problem. He earned the nickname "Speedy" in the early 1960s, when he made extremely fast ascents of some of the most difficult rock climbs in the French and Italian Alps. He's unshakable, utterly reliable, and can push hard day after day—vital expedition qualities. Now 36, he seemed as incorrigibly positive as ever. I was looking forward to climbing with him.

I didn't know Rusty very well, but found him chatty and deeply involved in a philosophy of his own. He is a tall, thin 41-year-old, a lecturer in the University of Calgary's Outdoor Pursuits programme. He has a soft South African accent, a quiet, almost shy, manner and, as his name suggests, rust-coloured hair and beard. I had first heard of Rusty when I was a young climber in England; he had made an early ascent of the North Face of the Eiger. He had also made a number of other difficult alpine ascents in Europe in the early 1960s. Rusty stopped in the little village in the valley bottom to take pictures, and Speedy and I continued up the wooded slope toward the monastery.

This trail I knew very well. I couldn't count the number of times I had been up and down it, both trekking and on expeditions. It's one of the most beautiful areas in the Khumbu. I've known the rhododendrons in spring, when their full-bloomed scent is unforgettable. But now, I noticed, in the dampness, they exuded a different fragrance. Damp leaves and pine needles were pressed underfoot as we wound slowly up the Tengboche hill. Just below the top, we crossed under the low arch that signifies the entrance to a sacred place. Mounting the gentle grassy mound of the monastery grounds, we had a commanding view of the Dudh Kosi valley and the Indian plains in the distance. It was a fitting vantage point for the most important monastery in the area. We were given a bunkhouse and cooking area, and we had our lunch. Afterwards, we filed quietly into the central chamber, where brightly coloured *thankas* (embroidered paintings) hung on the low lit walls, and rows of Tibetan prayer books were arranged behind the head lama, Nawang Tenzing Zang-Po. He was seated cross-legged on a Tibetan carpet, his

sacred instruments and receptacles at hand. On the far side of the room, a number of pigeonhole slots held more Tibetan prayer books. We were given tea and biscuits, the sign of welcome. The lama sat quietly chanting, punctuating his tones with drums and cymbals as he blessed the container of rice. Both the Sherpas and the Westerners stepped forward to receive *katas,* or white prayer scarves, around their necks.

After we had filed out, some Sherpas who had collected other charms in the form of little nylon necklaces, appropriately blessed, went round to the team members and solemnly handed them out as extra protection. The Sherpas reminded us that the goddess of the mountain only allows us to climb it if she is pleased with us. If she is angry she will take lives. The goddess's favours can never be taken for granted and the Sherpas take this part of the ceremony very seriously. They have known too many who have been killed in the Khumbu Icefall or on the faces.

The following day, August 10, most people were up early, taking photographs of the magnificent scenery. Ama Dablam at 22,494 feet is the most prominent peak, but you can see Everest's summit over the crest of the Nuptse Ridge. The Canadian expedition members were beginning to realize what they had come to do. It wasn't far now.

I chatted with Lloyd "Kiwi" Gallagher, a 42-year-old alpine specialist for the Kananaskis Provincial Park in Alberta. He was the deputy leader and had as much high-altitude experience as anyone on the expedition. He had already climbed at altitudes above 23,000 feet on Pumo Ri in Nepal in 1977 and on Muztagata in China in the fall of 1981.

He is a congenial New Zealander with reddish fair hair and beard and the quiet but direct manner befitting a long and successful career as a mountain guide. I knew that Kiwi was past his technical prime, but I felt that his years of mountaineering administration and group leadership would be an asset to a group the size of the Canadian expedition.

I also took advantage of the time to get to know Bill March, the 40-year-old leader of the expedition. I had been acquainted with him in my early climbing days in Chamonix. I did not encounter him again, however, for ten years, when we re-met in Calgary in 1978, at the time he immigrated to Canada. He is a big man, over six feet tall and broad-shouldered, and he speaks in a slightly imposing style, in a broad London drawl. His main mark in the mountaineering world, other than as a guide or instructor, was made in the 1960s and 1970s in Scotland, where he pioneered a number of difficult ice climbs.

After moving to North America, Bill had done a good deal more rock climbing, putting up a number of new routes on the sandstone cliffs in Zion National Park in Utah and repeating a number of the longer

41

classical climbs of the late 1960s, including an ascent of The Nose of El Capitan in Yosemite Valley. In Canada, he had focussed most of his attention on instructing and had added to his already impressive list a number of Canadian frozen waterfalls. In his capacity as a guide Bill had taken parties to Mt. Mera (21,300 feet) in Nepal and several volcanic peaks of similar elevation in Mexico and Equador. Although these are not really challenging mountains, they had given him a taste of altitude. He also had been on expeditions to Dhaulaghiri IV and Nuptse. However limited some aspects of his experience, I considered him a stable, mature person, and thought that if anyone could draw the team together, it would be Bill.

From the heavily forested region of Tengboche, we descended to the Imja Kola and crossed a spectacular gorge on a small suspension bridge. From here we began to climb gradually toward the village of Pangboche. The vegetation became sparser, large trees giving way to scrub juniper, tundra, and wild flowers. Pangboche, one of the highest of the Sherpa settlements, was home to our Sherpa, Sungdare, whose previous two ascents of Everest had respectful recognition from our members. It was also the site of one of the oldest *gompas,* or monasteries, in the area, and was reputed to house the most spiritually powerful lama. We did not stop in then, but the place was to become a refuge for Bill March later on.

The climbers walked independently or in small groups, chatting; some were rejuvenating old relationships, others were getting to know newcomers. I was able to re-establish contact with three younger climbers from the Calgary area, James Blench, Dwayne Congdon, and Dave McNab, very active amateur climbers involved in mountaineering instruction. James, a slightly built 26-year-old bachelor, wore a full beard, hair hanging below his shoulders, and a golf cap, and exhibited an ironic, counter-cultural sense of humour. He is particularly skilled on waterfall ice, and had been above 24,000 feet on Ganga Purna in 1981, which put him just behind Roger and me in terms of previously achieved altitude. Dwayne, a quiet, clean-shaven 25-year-old, had also been to Ganga Purna, but because he had been sick he had never completed the climb. Dave, a tall, blond 26-year-old, was in a similar situation to Dwayne's: he had also been ill on Ganga Purna. I got along well with him. He is an open, jovial character, pleasant to be around.

Jim Elzinga, age 27, was a close friend of the above three. I considered him one of the strongest climbers on the expedition. He is 6 feet 4 inches and weighs 200 pounds, with strikingly light blond hair and boyish good looks. He looks more like my idea of a football player than a mountain climber. I had been on the South West Face of Mt. Logan with him in 1979 and on the 1981 expedition to Dhaulagiri I. I considered his greatest strength to be in the area of difficult alpine climbing. I felt he would be an asset to the expedition, but neither he nor I tried to hide various disagreements we had developed in recent years.

As we approached the village of Pheriche, the weather gradually closed in. The mountains were shrouded in mist and it began to rain lightly. Pheriche, at an altitude of almost 14,000 feet, used to boast a supply of scrub juniper, but the trees were gradually cut for firewood, and now it is barren and windy. The deforestation in these highland areas has led to a strict conservation programme, and no expeditions or trekkers are supposed to cut wood for cooking. Even the local people can only use deadwood. In the higher areas, in the yak huts, they often use dried yak dung for fires.

Up until 1980, wood was still used on expeditions and was a major source of income for the local people. Yak loads of firewood would be taken up to base camp and sold to expeditions. This has now been stopped. We hoped, with our propane bottles, to make as little impact on the environment as possible.

We stopped in the village for rest. It consisted of a wide main street, along which were ranged stone huts and small turf and rock-walled yak enclosures. The wind sweeping through the village added to the air of desolation.

In one of these huts, the atmosphere heightened by cold winds moaning in the rafters, one of the Sherpas explained that, contrary to Western understanding, there are in fact two kinds of Yeti: Miki, a cannibal, and Chuttee, a yak eater. Both, he said, are covered in long, dark hair, similar to the brown bear, which they sometimes resemble when they rear up clumsily. But he insisted that the Yeti normally crawl on all fours, in spite of our misconception (understandable in foreigners, he seemed to imply) that they walk upright. Apparently, the best evidence for deciding whether you are looking at a Miki or a Chuttee is whether it has just eaten your partner or your yak. At least, that would be the most reliable indication for a foreigner.

The nights were beginning to grow colder now. The expedition divided into small groups and we sat around smoky yak-dung fires and sipped warm rice chang. We realized that, with the extra few thousand feet of elevation, it would now be snowing in Base Camp.

Don Serl and I got a chance to talk that evening. He's a tall, thin, Vancouver mountaineer in his mid-thirties, with whom I had been on Annapurna IV in winter. He is a modest, likeable character.

I also exchanged news with Laurie Skreslet, a 32-year-old climber from Calgary. I had known Laurie ever since I first came to Canada in 1974. He is an intense character, frank about both his strong drives and

The lateral moraine merges
almost imperceptively with
the boulder-strewn surface
of the Khumbu glacier.

A view of Nupste from
the approach march to
Everest Base Camp. The
south face of this peak
was attempted as a
training climb in 1982 by
seven members of the
expedition.

his insecurities. He is a very strong ice climber and had climbed several peaks in Peru that were over 20,000 feet. I find him very likeable.

The morning of August 11 dawned clear, the glistening walls and ridges of Taweche and Lobuche Peak and the rock pinnacle of Cholatse soaring above, brilliantly etched against the dark blue of the rarified air. The face of Ama Dablam rose steeply out of the gorge of the Imja Kola, one of the most impressive faces in this area. Most of us took the day for rest and acclimatization. Some went for walks, others sipped tea or took photographs.

I spent some time with Dave Read, a tall, thin 33-year-old Yorkshireman with a ribald sense of humour, a very old friend of mine whom I had known since I was 16 years old.

I then went up onto the ridge below Nuptse. This area was very familiar to me. I had been here on the Everest winter expedition two years previously, and for trekking only the winter before. Now the snows had gone and the short scrub grass stretched up to the rocky slopes of the mountains. As I climbed slowly up the hillside, I could feel the altitude.

I find that if I climb high during the day and return to a lower elevation to sleep, eat, and rest, I maximize my performance. It permits the necessary physiological changes: a slow increase in the blood's red cells and haemoglobin content. But even this is only a temporary acclimatization; if the body is stressed continually, day after day, it begins to wear. Over time, everybody will lose weight and energy and eventually their health, unless they have lower altitude recuperation. This seems to be a very individual matter, with highly varied personal "ceilings." Where one person can rest and recuperate, another slowly wastes.

The following morning, now in a long line, we headed up a broad, sloping valley, then rightwards up a steep hill to Dugla on the terminal moraine of the Khumbu glacier. A path up the small valley bordering the moraine brought us to Lobuche, a tiny collection of yak huts offering shelter for trekkers—the final stepping-stone to Base Camp, with two new trekking lodges and a Russian-made solar shower. Lobuche is the limit of habitation, at the edge of the vast expanse of crumbled boulder and ice that leads to the heights beyond. On our way up, the place had a very simple, rustic and innocent air, very unlike the way it would seem later, when some of these men, now lazing around reading, chatting, drinking tea, and taking short walks, would feel as if their souls had been torn to pieces.

Laurie Skreslet expressed the eager mood of some of the climbers by walking up to Base Camp. He returned very tired and had to be given

Diamox to counter the effects of altitude. It's sometimes hard to realize at this stage the importance of a gradual build-up. We had two months to go, and would have to take it slowly.

On the morning of August 15, the expedition left Lobuche for Base Camp. High in the sky, a raven caught my eye, soaring playfully on the currents, sometimes closing its wings to dive like a bullet. My imagination immediately joined it, and enjoyed its overview: a line of people curving slowly up the Khumbu glacier, yak herders dressed in drab wool clothing, shouting encouragingly to heavily laden beasts. Bright colours —reds and yellows, blues and greens—as the file wound slowly up the ice. The raven was watching expectantly, I knew. This large expedition would be better than the small ones of Pumo Ri and Nuptse. There should be some good pickings—large amounts of wasted food, piles of garbage. In my mind, I heard the raven say, "It will be the same as all the big expeditions—they'll throw stones at me and the dogs will chase me away, but the Sherpas will remind the foreigners of my reincarnated soul, and I'll be all right."

As the sun warmed the air, the currents took the raven high up out of my sight. I immediately felt a loss—a loss of freedom, of flight. I felt imprisoned by innumerable yak loads of equipment, the complex intermeshing of so many people, the ever-present struggle of my body to acclimatize. I would rather be a raven.

A REAL WORLD OF FANTASY

BASE CAMP was set on tumbled moraine boulders and dirty glacial ice, a small tent city reminiscent of something out of the Klondike Gold Rush. Peter Spear, Dave McNab and the Sherpas had done an incredible job. Base Camp tents, cook tents, and stone walls roofed with large tarpaulins were everywhere. Smaller tents for Sherpas and climbers were scattered on small rock platforms seeming to ride the waves of the turbulent icefall. We all shook hands and slapped one another on the back. There was an optimistic air. We were really here. The weather was fine, Base Camp was already established, and it was only August 15.

From our scattered jumble of boulders, ice, and moraine, the eye was drawn upward, to their source, the Khumbu Icefall. This was to be our first objective, a tumbling chaotic ocean of ice, flowing between the steep icy walls of Everest's West Ridge and the North Face of Nuptse. It had claimed many lives in the past 30 years. For now, it was more pleasant to imbibe the hot tea, and enjoy the camaraderie and the optimism of our new camp.

*Pumori (23,442') viewed
from the summit of Gorak
Shep. This viewpoint is a
favorite trekking peak for
people visiting the Everest
Base Camp.*

Gradually, the slower climbers drifted in and each was given a tent. A military-style equipment issue followed, with brightly coloured clothing, gleaming carabiners, and new harnesses finding owners among Westerners and Sherpas.

On the morning of August 16, the Sherpas gathered for prayers. A flagpole and three long strings of prayer flags were erected to protect Base Camp from malevolent spirits. The Sherpas built a small stone altar upon which to burn juniper, mornings and evenings, so that this sweet-smelling smoke could also protect the camp and climbers. For the Sherpas this was a very important ceremony. Rice, chang, beer and whiskey were set upon the altar. The Sherpas sat immobile, chanting, while Westerners stumbled among them on the moraine, panting from the altitude, taking photographs. I felt they were a little oblivious to the solemnity of the occasion, in their fascination with the picturesque qualities of the ceremony. A celebration followed, in which chang, beer, and Canadian whiskey were raised in a toast to the success of the expedition and the safety of its many members.

In the afternoon we attended a similar ceremony at the Catalan camp nearby, which was to protect them while climbing the West Ridge of Everest. At this unaccustomed elevation alcohol brings quick euphoria. Thus a collection of rather drunken climbers staggered back to the Canadian tents for a late lunch. Many collapsed in a stupor in the afternoon, but I perceived this as the correct state of mind in which to undergo a minor operation on an ingrown toenail, especially as I cannily observed that Dr. Jones was not as drunk as I.

Dr. Jones seemed a tremendous man to have along. He is 50 years old, grey-haired, and has a face that wrinkles warmly into a smile. He had been to Nepal before, on the British-Nepalese Army expedition to Annapurna I, and had also been on expeditions to Iceland, Greenland, and Antarctica. He had experience in makeshift surgery, and I was very impressed with the work he did on my big toe in these rough surroundings. I held my bottle in a tight embrace throughout. At the end I understood him to say I should stay off the foot a few days to give it a chance to heal (he was hard to understand in his state!)

As people slowly adapted to base camp altitude, they began to work their way through a long list of chores that needed doing—hanging stoves were assembled, personal crampons fitted, boxes opened and inventoried, and ladders assembled. It rained every afternoon and snowed every evening. Three inches of snow during the night was a prelude to the wintery mornings.

On August 18, the first group moved up into the icefall for a reconnaissance. Speedy Smith, Bill March, Dave McNab, and Laurie

Skreslet, accompanied by four of the most experienced Sherpas, went leftwards under the seracs of the Lho La and onto the steepening icefall on the left-hand side. After a gain of almost 1,000 feet, they traversed between huge unstable blocks across to easier ground in the centre of the icefall. The intense heat of late morning brought them back down, with a report on the number of ladders that would be needed.

Bill noted in his diary:

It is really now an exciting time because we're really on the verge of making the mountaineering decisions—the route through the icefall. It's the kind of thing that all the climbers are looking forward to. They are all men of experience; they're all giving valuable input into this difficult decision and we feel we're on home ground at last. No more walking into the tropical rain and the leeches and the interminable ridges of up and down, up and down. There is only one way now, and that's up, up the icefall, up the Western Cwm, up the South Pillar if we can. And then, on to the summit.

The "if we can" was significant, in that the Canadian Everest expedition's first objective had been a challenging, unclimbed pillar on Everest's south flank, which George Kinnear had publicly dubbed "the Canadian Spur" shortly after he became leader. Unfortunately, in the spring of 1980 the Canadian Spur was climbed by a Polish expedition and became known henceforth as "the Polish Pillar." This embarrassment was overcome by the invention of a 1,200 foot possible variation on the Polish Pillar, which was then freshly presented to the Canadian public and sponsors as the Canadian Spur. This was now the objective. However, a final decision on the actual route would not have to be made until above Camp III, at 23,000 feet. From that point it would be possible to change the objective to the already climbed Polish route or to traverse rightwards onto the easier ground of the normal South Col route (the route taken by the 1981 American Medical expedition).

Optimism is a desirable quality, but a dash of realism is also sometimes useful. The team's high-altitude record holder, other than me, had just been sent home, leaving a wealth of lower-altitude technical and alpine experience that by no means transferred painlessly into the realm of extended high-altitude expedition climbing.

That afternoon it rained again and the mist descended, cutting off our view of the mountains above. In the afternoon we listened to avalanches roaring down somewhere on Everest, Nuptse, and Pumo Ri, while we sorted out equipment and ladders and recovered from the exertion of the

day. Each evening it snowed, and each day the sun loosened the new snow and avalanches poured down the slopes.

Later that afternoon, Stephen Bezruchka arrived, having travelled independently. He is a tall, thin ascetic-looking medical doctor experienced in Third World medicine and the author of a book about trekking in Nepal. He had signed on as our high altitude doctor, and he also had varied general mountaineering experience to his credit.

The following day, a group of four more climbers completed the previous traverse and reached a small plateau, seamed with only an occasional crevasse. At Base Camp, the preparation and assembly of equipment continued. One-third of the expedition was now down with some form of dysentery. We hoped this would be reduced with the completion of our water-supply system.

On August 20, seven climbers and a number of Sherpas again headed into the icefall. Speedy led a ladder team, including James Blench and Blair Griffiths, to bridge sections of the traverse. By midday they had already fixed nine bridges, and they descended to the lower section of the icefall where Jim Elzinga had fixed two and Don Serl one. In the meantime, Bill and Laurie and two trail-breaking Sherpas pushed a route up a wide, shallow low-angled snow valley to a serac wall at its head. From here they got the first glimpse up into the Western Cwm (pronounced "Coom").

Bill noted:

Everyone was in good spirits at our rate of progress, and Laurie and I with Gyaljen Sirdar and a second Sherpa reached the head of the valley. From here there were two possible routes, one straight up, which looked very threatened by seracs, and another trending diagonally right up an indefinite ramp system. We split up, with Laurie and I climbing right and Gyaljen and partner moving straight up. Laurie and I could see the final ice cliff barring our access to the Western Cwm. As we approached it, we found it was necessary to cross a chaotic collapsed area of jumbled ice blocks, threatened by a huge 80–foot-high ship's prow of ice. We called this section "the graveyard"! In actual fact, it was easy to cross, but the way to the Western Cwm was barred by an ice cliff nearly 30 feet high. I offered to take the lead and slowly front-pointed my way up the rather sugary ice. At the top the serac was crumbling snow. I cut a slot and shinnied up. We were at the top of the icefall! Laurie followed and we shook hands, grinning like a couple of Cheshire cats. I felt highly privileged to be in this almost sacred place. It felt as if the door had been opened on Everest and the greatest dangers were behind us. Three days through the icefall was really good going.

On August 22, a group of four led by Tim Auger pushed the route beyond "the Prow" and immediately ran into large crevasses requiring bridges. Speedy's engineering corps followed hotly behind, and by midday the route was completed all the way to Camp I. Most of the group returned to Base Camp early, leaving Speedy and the Sherpa, Nuru, to finish off. Speedy commented about Nuru: "He is very good with bridges and I'm very impressed. His familiarity with much of the icefall equipment is far in advance of most of the climbers. He has already been on many expeditions which have come through the icefall."

Now that the route was finished to Camp I we had a problem. We were not allowed to establish Camp I until September 1, official opening of the post-monsoon period. So for the next two days the concentration was on pushing beyond Camp I in an effort to find a route to Camp II, and on stocking Camp I with many of the loads required for higher on the mountain. On August 23, the Sherpas moved up 10 loads.

Peter Spear related his part in this work:

It was quite an eerie experience walking up the Khumbu Icefall in the dark. There are so many strange objects, shapes as you move up. Because we were wearing headlamps, you have a little beam of light in front of you, perhaps 10 or 12 feet wide, depending on how high you lift your head, and everything else around is pitch black. As you walk along the fixed line you have to find the knots to find out where the ropes are tied together, unclip your carabiner [snaplink] from your safety loop, then clip it on above the knot to keep moving up. When you reach a bridge across the crevasse, it is quite an interesting experience, because due to the steepness of the climb everyone is wearing crampons, and we are crossing aluminum ladders with one safety line, which we clip our carabiner to, and one hand line which we use for balance. You have 20 feet of aluminum ladder stretched in front of you, a little pool of light in front of you, and a hole perhaps as deep as 100 feet below you. You very carefully get your crampons to match the rungs of the ladder and very slowly and carefully move across these ladders. Some of the ladders are horizontal, some of them rise at a 45 degree angle. . . . As we move up the Khumbu Glacier, big tall seracs of ice catch the gleam of your headlight beam and make it a real world of fantasy.

In the foreground, the Canadian Mount Everest Expedition Base Camp showing the kitchen/dining tent and the equipment dump. In the background, the tents of the Catalan expedition, which was attempting the west ridge of Everest, are dwarfed by the summit of Pumori.

The Khumbu icefall dominates the frail string of prayer flags and the rising smoke of smoldering juniper boughs. The boughs were burnt daily by the Sherpas to appease Chomolungma, *"Goddess Mother of the Land."*

The alter at Base Camp showing Sherpa offerings of food and drink to Chomolungma. *In the Sherpa culture the mountains are often deified.*

Laurie Skreslet attaches a flag to the line of flags fluttering in the wind at Base Camp. The Sherpas believe that each time a flag is stirred by the wind a prayer inscribed on it is offered up to the mountain gods.

Peter Spear, the highly efficient Base Camp manager, prepares loads of equipment for transportation through the icefall. Peter was completely buried in the avalanche which killed the three Sherpas and was saved only by the prompt action of his teammate Rusty Baillie.

Team picture. The team consisted of sixteen climbers, five support personnel and twenty-nine high altitude Sherpas.

"RECONNAISSANCE" CAMP

AUGUST 24 was my first day on the mountain. Bill, Blair, Speedy, and I, along with four Sherpas, left at 2:00 a.m., equipped with a map that Tim had drawn of the route beyond Camp I. (The reason for going out in the early hours of the morning was that the glacier was least active at that time, and there was less chance of an avalanche.) The weather was terrible—snow in big, wet flakes. As we made our way through Base Camp, following the uneven trail past the altar, the prayer flags flapped softly in the morning breeze. Each person's headlamp cast a circle of light that left him to move in a dream-like world of his own.

When we arrived at the foot of the fixed ropes, there were six or seven inches of new snow. I moved to the front to pull the ropes onto the surface. The four Sherpas were behind us. I could see their lights just leaving Base Camp. Speedy was close behind me.

As I approached the traverse, I heard the rumble of an avalanche over on the left. As the rumble continued, I looked down for Bill's head lamp. I didn't see it, but the roar subsided and I felt that everyone must be in the clear. (Bill told me afterwards he had actually felt the wind from the avalanche as it passed down to his left.)

We were able to move through the traverse quite quickly on good trail, well-placed ropes, and secure bridges. The rope now ran all the way to Camp I, and each person moved independently with a sliding jumar clamp on the rope or, as I often did, with a carabiner clipped over as a running belay. (This device allowed us in following days to retrieve at least one wriggling climber from the hoary depths of a crevasse.)

As it became light, the Sherpas caught up with us and shared the trail-breaking. Because of the fresh snow, it took four-and-a-half hours to reach Camp I. Still, I felt fine. At Camp I, we dug out loads to retrieve the equipment and ladders we would need to fix bridges up the center of the Western Cwm. Once equipped, the four of us and three Sherpas pushed on above Camp I. By 10:30 a.m. we had fixed a number of ladders up the centre of the Cwm. At that time, we decided that the bad visibility and deep snow warranted a descent.

On our return the others stayed at the Camp I site to eat their packed lunches. I didn't feel hungry and I wanted to keep going down so I set off by myself. As I descended through the icefall I contemplated its dangers. I was very concerned about the possibility of avalanches off the west shoulder. Bill March noted his concern at the same time:

The big problem with the icefall is that on either side of this moving, hanging glacier are the steep slopes of Nuptse and the west flank of Everest, and from these very steep slopes threaten hanging cliffs or seracs and also open snow slopes, which after a heavy fall will avalanche and will sweep the left- and right-hand side of the icefall . . . obviously, it may be under certain conditions, very heavy snow, the route will be closed. It will be completely unjustifiable to force our way through the icefall. We're just going to hope that the good weather we've had the last few days will hold and that we'll be able eventually to find a safer possible way through the icefall.

I didn't say anything because I felt a little guilty about not being able to help earlier, when I was recovering from my toe operation, and didn't want people to think I was being lazy or too assertive.

An hour later I arrived at the foot of the icefall and unclipped from the last fixed rope. Suddenly a huge explosion from the Lho La jerked my attention to the wall above, to a collapsed serac now crashing in a huge avalanche towards me.

I started to run and covered 100 exhausting yards as the wind swept past me. I kept walking, shaken, gradually enjoying the sensation of heart and lungs returning to normal. Bill came in one hour after me and said that he had been even closer to another avalanche that roared down from the Lho La. We decided to look for an alternate route to the start of our fixed ropes. Tim Auger went out the following day and marked a route with flagged bamboo wands. In actual fact, however, we never used this longer, alternate route at all and accepted the risk of the Lho La's occasional serac fall.

Bad weather continued. In fact, by August 25 it was the worst since we had arrived at Base Camp. We spent the time under cover in "teams" of two, busy on what I tended to regard as "make work" projects but which were in fact vital work for a large expedition.

On days like this, I found myself creeping around, trying to be invisible, because the atmosphere was a cross between Santa's workshop and the sort of large industrial plant where you feel surreptitious going to the bathroom or going for a coffee without a piece of paper or some part of something in your hand. Peter would inevitably catch you and ask if you wouldn't mind helping with a whole clipboard of little jobs, such as issuing gear, assembling stoves, shock cording tent poles, checking oxygen systems, counting and racking carabiners, cutting fixed rope into 300 foot lengths, moving tents from one pile of rubble to a flatter one, pushing precarious-looking boulders off pedestals of ice;

James Blench, an instructor from the Yamnurka Mountain School, conducts an ice climbing course for the high altitude Sherpas. Although many of the Sherpas were competent climbers, schools were held to standardize technique and evaluate relative climbing ability.

sorting, re-sorting, stacking and re-stacking boxes of food and gear, rebuilding rock walls, and checking out water and sewage systems.

In fact, early in the morning, when you made your way to the large A-frame kitchen tent in the snow and mist and dark, surrounded by heaps of stone and rubble, and entered its bright interior, the impression of being on a construction site was so pervasive that you expected to hear the bulldozers start up. We jokingly referred, over coffee, to imaginary heavy machinery and earth-moving projects.

In truth, of course, the Base Camp operation was no small matter. Peter's gang managed to keep a small town functioning, on a constantly moving foundation that was shaken periodically by nearby avalanches, and which often fell victim to the complete, unexpected collapse of huge stone walls weighing tons and tons, the sudden fall of house-sized boulders, and the incessant groan and crack of the bottomless ice underfoot.

August 26 was the "day of the big carry." Almost everyone on the expedition earned points on Peter's load list. Those who earned the most points, it was generally believed, earned the best chance at the summit. The spirit of that day was a half-serious competitiveness mixed with general enthusiasm. This feeling was expressed by Tim Auger: "You could compare your performance to the other guys. Some guys were fairly rapidly cutting time off their trips up the icefall. Whereas, other people were quite a few hours behind them. You could gauge yourself that way."

Frankly, I enjoy speed for its own sake. When you're well-tuned, it feels great. Also, considering the treacherous aspects of the icefall, it was probably safer. The prospect of returning, mildly exerted, at 8:00 a.m. after work well done, is always a satisfying inducement to me.

So we were all up at 2:30 in the morning, keen to make points. People left at various times from 3:00 a.m. onwards, headlights carving through the darkness. Most of the climbers were carrying two oxygen bottles, while some who felt they were not yet strong enough only carried one. The Sherpas carried 55 pounds each. As I left I could see dancing bright specks already on the fixed ropes in the icefall—two Sherpas and Jim Elzinga, who had left earlier without loads, in order to break trail and pull clear the ropes. Some others were ahead of me too.

I followed the trail as my light picked it out. My load weighed heavily, but I pressed on until I caught up with the Sherpas in front of me. Then I tucked in behind them, plodding on to their comforting mantras. Gradually we caught up with more Sherpas as they waited to cross ladders. We made our way like this, stop and start, until we reached the end of the crevassed traverse. Then the way was more open and we could pass others.

Peter Hillary, leader of the New Zealand Lhotse south face expedition which shared Base Camp with the Canadian expedition, contemplates atop a serac perch near Base Camp.

The central section of the icefall which moved downhill roughly a metre a day. This was to many climbers the most dangerous part of the climb.

By the time we arrived at the Prow and the rope ladder up to the plateau, however, there was more congestion. Sherpas were waiting to go up one at a time, under the menacing towers of ice that seemed to lean in on all sides. However, there was fun and energy in the air, shouts up the ladder to hurry, an occasional snowball, jokes, laughter.

Rusty came elbowing his way through, jumped the line, and almost caused a riot. We spent a long time awaiting our turn, but finally were able to move out. Twenty minutes later we caught up with Jim Elzinga and the lead Sherpas, and then our speed was reduced to a crawl as the Sherpas broke trail.

When we arrived at Camp I we stamped down a place for the loads, put them underneath a huge tarpaulin, and headed back down. I joined an eager crowd of 10 or 15 Sherpas waiting at the top of the fixed rope for the upcoming parties to unclip, clearing the way for the descent. As soon as they did, we grabbed the rope and swooped down, peels of laughter and shouts of abuse following us. "Ghengis Khan and his hordes!" shouted Speedy as we hurtled past. We unclipped above climbers who were panting under their loads, hanging on their jumars, and clipped on again below them to keep charging down.

Staggering, out of breath, Lhakpa Tshering laughing hard on my heels, I rushed the last few hundred yards to Base. It had only taken us 50 minutes down, four hours for the round trip. Up on the icefall I could still see figures making their way upwards to Camp I. We tucked into a hearty breakfast.

THE HIGHEST VALLEY IN THE WORLD

LATER ON August 26, my twin brother Adrian arrived with the New Zealand Lhotse Expedition, made up of Peter Hillary, (son of the famous Edmund); Paul Moores, with whom I had done much climbing; Fred From ("Fred From Australia," as they called him) and my brother. It was good to see him again. We had shared a long apprenticeship for the work at hand.

We started at the age of 15 on the gritstone outcrops near home in Yorkshire, progressed through Britain's classical Lake District and Snowdonia technical rock faces, then northwards to the rigours of Scottish ice. At the age of 17 we made our debut on the "difficult" class of faces of the European Alps. Over the next eight seasons, Chamonix became a second home, from which we climbed many of the north faces in France, Switzerland, and Italy.

In 1973, at the age of 23, we drove a small van across Asia to the Kulu Himalaya and made the first ascent of the technically difficult West Face of Ali Ratna Tibba, "alpine style." This ascent was to set the tone for many of our future climbs, especially as we expanded our geographical boundaries toward the "super" alpine areas of Alaska, Patagonia, Bolivia, and Peru.

In 1979, with a small close-knit team of friends, we failed at 23,000 feet on the 26,000-foot Annapurna II. The following year we reached a short distance below the summit of Nanga Parbat, where we were driven back by the first violent storms of the monsoon.

Adrian and I stayed in Nepal after the Everest West Ridge attempt to join the Canadian Dhaulagiri expedition. Six weeks later, we were fortunate enough to stand on the summit of Canada's first 8,000-metre peak. This expedition did not use oxygen and the six-man team was at that time the smallest group ever to climb the mountain.

Paul Moores, too, had been on the Annapurna II and the Nanga Parbat climbs and I had also done a lot of climbing with him in the Alps. So the New Zealand expedition members were no strangers to me.

They had no Sherpas, so when Tim and I started over to help them, Dawa Dorje arranged for several Sherpas to join us. Within an hour or so we had built their tent platforms in the rubble. Compared to our expedition, theirs was tiny: a mere 40 or 50 loads arrived with them on yaks. They seemed to have travelled well and had arrived relaxed and confident. We had an enjoyable dinner with them that night in our camp.

August 27 began as related by Tim Auger:

> The climbers turned out and had their breakfast. I went over to the Sherpa tent to see what was going on. I found them all sitting around the tent very quietly, just sitting there. I realized that there was some reason that they didn't feel like going. I went back and told the climbers that the Sherpas were over there sitting tight and I had a hunch they had some reason.

I awoke at four o'clock (late enough to avoid line-ups in the icefall). On my way to the cook tent I was impressed by a layer of new snow and enormous wet flakes reflected in my headlamp. Obviously there would be no carry today. But when I got to the cook tent I found people milling around, some complete with harnesses, ice axes, rucksacks, and headlamps. Somebody said, "The Sherpas are all sitting around and don't look like they want to go out today."

"Well, what do you expect?" I replied. "Look at it. Has anybody gone?"

They knew Rusty Baillie and some Sherpas had, but weren't sure about others. Kiwi Gallagher came in and immediately gathered what was happening. "We've got to stop them!" I said, and sensed immediate agreement from Kiwi and Tim. Kiwi grabbed a radio and shot outside to stop more Sherpas from leaving, then called Rusty.

There was no response. No one knew whether Rusty had a radio. Kiwi ran up the moraine to a vantage point and shouted towards the lights he could see in the distance. Rusty shouted back, got the message, and acknowledged it. Shouts in Sherpa further up were followed by a movement downward of the spots of light that we could see from Base Camp. So at least we knew the abort was accomplished.

Reactions in camp were varied, the doubts reinforced by a concurrent improvement in the weather. Many members, I knew, felt we had over-reacted and wasted a valuable day.

Later that day Bill called another meeting, at which three things were decided. One: We wouldn't make a carry if there was heavy snow at Base Camp. Two: "go" or "no go" would be determined by Bill or Kiwi. Three: a Westerner with a radio would go in front of groups of Sherpas to monitor and report changing conditions and to be in a position to prevent any Sherpas from continuing.

I was glad to see an official policy established, and also relieved that our position was vindicated by more snowfall after the meeting. As Speedy recorded, "Snows most of the day. Avalanches roaring down all of the mountains, noisier than usual and the moraine starts creaking as well."

Although regulations forbade occupancy of Camp I before September 1, Bill reached agreement with our accompanying Nepalese Liaison Officer that a "reconnaissance" camp (on the Camp I site) would be permitted so that we could monitor movement through the icefall and up to Camp II. Although it was snowing very hard the following morning, August 28, we got 20 Sherpas and 14 climbers through to Camp I, re-breaking trail and repairing bridges. The next day, Bill March, Tim Auger, Dave McNab and I, accompanied by four Sherpas—Sungdare, Nawang Karma, Gyaljen Phortse and Tenzing Tashi—moved up to Camp I to stay.

Kiwi Gallagher wrote: "Hopefully we can start getting a better feel for the mountain and a better reading on weather by staying at this altitude of 19,600 feet." We were now beginning to grapple seriously with the mountain. The real work was underway. The prime task now would be to stock Camp I, and the bulk of the loads for higher up would now have to go through the icefall.

Steve Bezruchka, the expedition's high altitude doctor, carefully makes his way across an exposed ladder bridge in the traverse section of the icefall.

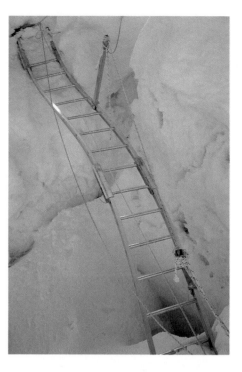

Team member crossing a ladder in the area of the fatal serac collapse in which Blair Griffiths was killed and two Sherpas injured.

A twin ladder, 16' long, compressed by the immense shifting force within the icefall. This ladder spanned a crevasse in the treacherous traverse section of the icefall.

Dave Read carrying a camera tripod across a ladder bridge. Dave, together with Pat Morrow, did much of the video filming after the death of Blair Griffiths.

Two climbers make their way along the fixed ropes spanning the crevasses in the upper section of the icefall. Above the immense face of Nuptse rises the spawning ground of avalanches which threatened the south side of the Western Cwm.

The high altitude Sherpa cook, Pemba Tsering, carrying a load in the upper icefall in the heavily crevassed zone just below Camp I. Behind, a second Sherpa carrys a ladder destined for the Western Cwm.

A climber crosses a ladder bridge spanning a deep crevasse in the icefall. For all of the team members, carrying heavy loads and wearing crampons, such crossings took a considerable amount of care and concentration—two factors greatly affected by altitude.

Rusty Baillie crossing a snow bridge at the Prow of the icefall. This immense, detached block of ice, the size of a large house, threatened the exit from the icefall.

Gordon Smith in the lower icefall at night. Travel through the icefall was mainly at night and early morning when the snow was hard.

I never got used to going through the icefall. I think anyone who claimed to cross it without fear was deceiving himself. At the beginning of the traverse, before my conscious mind could even take stock of the situation, an unconscious premonition would set my adrenalin flowing and my heart beating faster, and I would feel a queasy tightening in my gut. As I crossed, I was constantly aware of delicately poised tons of sheer blue ice, hanging, hardly in check, all around me. It took control to concentrate on extricating the stubborn rope, or to balance my crampons on the aluminum bridge, or to balance on a fine snow ridge.

Once at the end of the traverse, my mood changed. Now it wasn't tensely poised ice blocks, but a quieter, more remote threat of avalanche from the west shoulder of Everest. The glistening walls hung thousands of feet above me, and here, in "the valley," the floor was smoother, blasted clean by previous tons of churning power.

Then, the third stage, beyond the huge ice block we knew as the Canmore Hotel. In the traverse, the blocks were car-sized. Here, they were the size of buildings, but crazy, teetering, scattered misshapen ones. The evidence of violent structural change was everywhere, a vast, slow powerful tension. It was no place for bravado or false pretense. Just move. Move fast, and hope the place stayed quiet, just long enough to get to that rope ladder at the Prow, which led up and out to safety.

The weather didn't ease; fresh snow covered yesterday's tracks each morning. The heavy, smooth mounds of snow seemed to loom higher on the seracs and crevasse lips as the days went by.

On August 29, the morning we moved into our "reconnaissance camp," we assembled and erected tents, and still had time to mark out some trail for the following day. Several days of snowfall had packed over it, with only some marker wands still visible. We got in a couple hours of trail-breaking, then returned to our new home.

I tented with Tim Auger. Nawang Karma and Tenzing Tashi camped next to us, and one tent over were Bill March and Dave McNab. A few feet higher and behind, a fourth tent held Gyaljen Phortse and Sungdare.

Just after daybreak on August 30, all of us set out to find a route to Camp II. We wanted to stay as close as possible to the centre of the cwm, away from the avalanche threat of the sidewalls. We started with a series of sweeping zigzags through crevasses, but the way gradually evolved into a more direct line, well to the centre. This held up for a while, but we were gradually forced right again as we approached a new network of crevasses. We split into two teams to better our chances of finding a route. The crevasses became enormous—great gaping, lateral ones, reaching from the West Ridge of Everest to the North Face of Nuptse. Our two groups were forced together again at a point near the

"Nuptse Corner," an avalanche-swept corner of the glacier that touches the North Face of Nutpse. This was the gateway. Once past it, it was easier going, a wide snowfield across which we navigated on a heading to the Camp II site. We found it on the moraine on the glacier's true right, almost two miles above the corner.

The site was littered from previous expeditions, and there were many empty cans with strange Slavic markings among the junk. The Sherpas automatically checked them out for salvage. I found a tin of quite passable anchovies, which Bill refused to share. I felt quite insulted, but not enough to spoil my appetite.

Having established territoriality, we descended in the softening snow, under gathering cloud. Lower down, on snowshoes, still roped together, we entered white-out. We picked our way from wand to wand, their fluttering orange tags leading us through worsening wind and blowing snow to Camp I. We found the tents straining under the fresh snow. We cleared them off, climbed inside, and got the stoves going.

The mist cleared a little later in the day, but the snow fell steadily. We drank quantities of soup and tea, and fell asleep to the steady patter of snow on the tent, the pressing shadow of snow gradually creeping up the walls.

AVALANCHE

I LAY BARELY AWAKE, just aware of a weak light and cold air in the narrow, frosted opening of my sleeping bag. The radio crackled somewhere in the background, in a neighbouring tent. The noise drew my thoughts together. I realized that I was in Camp I. I could see now that the tent was bent under a lot of new snow, its dark shadow a third of the way up the walls. The radio crackled again and I could hear Bill March's muffled voice, which meant it was two tents over. I tried to understand the significance of this. He had to be speaking to Base Camp. Or maybe people in the icefall. But no. There wouldn't be people in the icefall. Or could there be? There seemed to be a lot of snow. For some minutes, I listened, catching the odd word here and there, and slowly I realized that he *was* talking to a carry. So they had left Base! I sat up and, feeling the altitude, immediately took a few deep breaths. I unzipped the door and forced by head out, frost condensation falling around my shoulders. Snow fell inside the tent. There must have been 18 inches of new snow at Camp I. Now I began to take in the seriousness of the problem Bill could be trying to deal with on the radio. How long ago might people have left Base Camp? My watch said

The chaos of the central
section of the traverse.
Climbers would pass
through this highly
unstable section of the
icefall as fast as possible.

A climber descending the
Prow on rapelle to the
bottom of the crevasse.
The crevasse floor was
made up of jammed blocks
of ice which some climbers
referred to as the
graveyard.

5:15. They could be two hours into the icefall by now! Maybe too late to turn back! But maybe there was less snow below—maybe there was *none* in Base Camp. I heard Kiwi Gallagher's voice. I couldn't understand much, but I did hear something about "no snow at Base," and some discussion about personnel locations. More reports came in, filling in gaps in my mental picture of the situation, until I realized that Sherpas and climbers were spread right through the middle of the icefall, over two hours in, and still over two hours from the top. Pat Morrow was in the lead, above "the valley" and was into snow so deep that he was requesting trail-breaking assistance down from Camp I. They had been lured into a vulnerable situation, and were now pushing upwards to get out of it.

I pulled my head back into the tent. Tim Auger was lying in his sleeping bag next to me, and I could see that he was waking. I was about to tell him about our probable recruitment as trail-breakers, when, strangely, I lost the thread of my thought. I wanted to say something to him but couldn't find words, as a new, uneasy feeling took over completely. Something was wrong. Tim sat up, blinking, listening, looking at nothing. I heard an avalanche. It kept going, getting louder. The tent started to shake. Tim and I looked at each other, as the floor shuddered and air blast snapped and tore deafeningly at the walls. It was a big one. Very big. In the roar, Tim's lips moved inaudibly, his eyes large, but I didn't answer. I just stared back at him, my entire consciousness flooded with the roar. It seemed a long time until, with a hollow rattle like distant thunder, it stopped. A very heavy, eerie silence returned. Tim and I were still rigid, staring at each other.

We both shouted to Bill, but immediately heard the radio. Pat Morrow. He said that he had almost been caught in the avalanche. He said that they were above it, but it went lower down. He thought that there were some Sherpas behind but he didn't know how many.

The radio was now crackling wildly. It was impossible, as we hurriedly pulled on boots and gear, to tell who was speaking. Somebody was saying that Base Camp got air blast too. God! It *must* have been big! Pat was going down to count people. Other voices spoke hurriedly, shouting words that we couldn't understand, but then, quickly, Kiwi's voice and others were imposing order. I realized that they were mobilizing from Base Camp for a search.

Once equipped, I went across to the Sherpa tent to explain to them what was going on, or at least what little I knew. Bill was standing nearby, now fully equipped, the radio at his hood. As I passed, he glanced at me, and our eyes shared our fears. Dave McNab was in their tent door, dressed and buckling on crampons. Then Rusty Baillie came on the radio, his voice clear but halting, explaining that there had been Sherpas above him, but they must certainly now be dead. He couldn't see anymore. The avalanche had actually hit him and he had been covered up to the waist. Peter Spear had also been covered, but they had found him again.

The radio messages were now clear and precise. Kiwi was co-ordinating from Base Camp, and teams were moving up quickly. Bill told me to stay with Sungdare, who had a touch of snow blindness and was ill, and Gyaljen Phortse. Bill, Dave, Pat, Nawang Karma and Tenzing Tashi clipped onto the rope and disappeared over the snow crest, down into the icefall.

This left me alone at Camp I with the two Sherpas and no radio. Sungdare and Gyaljen Phortse were in the tent just behind mine, 20 yards up the hill. I made my way up, knee deep in snow, and called from outside their door. They unzipped and let me in. Sungdare, a tall, confident, experienced mountaineer, was lying on his side, his knees pulled up and his arms across his face. Snow blindness is painful and illness is discouraging, but I knew he was feeling more than that. Gyaljen Phortse sat staring at the wall. Normally he was an effusive and friendly person, but now his eyes were dead and expressionless. All he said was, "When it snows like this we should be in Base Camp." There was nothing to say in reply.

I changed their gas cartridge and made them some tea. I had Sungdare roll around and sit up to check his eyes and alertness. He appeared to be all right. I suspected that, even before the avalanche, it had been his instincts and experience that had made him feel too sick to go out on a dangerous morning. Such illness can be a polite Sherpa statement of opinion on objective hazards.

I worked outside for a while, digging out the tents and gear and restacking equipment, and then went back into my own tent to make some breakfast, drink some tea, and contemplate the situation. I wondered how the team would react if there had been deaths or serious injuries. I thought, too, of the Sherpas I knew well from other expeditions, and hoped they were all right. In particular, I hoped that Pema Dorje was in the clear, because I knew his anxious mother had pleaded with him not to join our expedition.

Some of my thoughts were practical. We were racing the seasonal jet stream, which was coming lower every day now. At some point it would reach the 29,028 foot level of Everest's summit, and we had to get there first. I made calculations: the speed of loads through the icefall and up to the camps. Only so many backs to carry them, only so many days to do it. One day it might snow too much. Maybe two days. Maybe a week.

The scene of the avalanche where Pasang Sona's body was recovered. The crossed ski poles mark the site. On the extreme left, life-link avalanche probes used to locate the body stick out of the snow.

Steve Bezruchka supervises the administration of CPR to Pasang Sona while Rusty Baillie attempts body rewarming.

Where could we draw the line? How long could we use up resources and time before we even got out of Base Camp? Maybe we had been pushing too hard. But maybe there was no other way to succeed.

A few hours later Tim Auger, David McNab, and two Sherpas returned. They were very subdued. The Sherpas went to Sungdare and Gyaljen Phortse's tent, and Tim and Dave came into mine. I began to prepare tea and food for them.

"All the Westerners are OK," Tim said. That was good to hear. But Tim continued, "Some Sherpas have been killed. We dug out one body. Pasang Sona. They spent an hour, Steve [Dr. Stephen Bezruchka] and Rusty, trying to revive him. But it wasn't any use. They thought there were two others missing, but they couldn't be sure till they did a real check at Base. They'll radio up when they know who."

The avalanche had covered acres with a compressed mixture of snow and ice blocks, so that as the recovery teams clambered through a landscape of teetering, crevassed devastation, in falling snow and grey cold, almost every probing pole hit something hard. After a time, their sense of desperate urgency became deadened; eventually they realized that they had been lucky to find Pasang Sona because of a visible piece of rope that led to him. It was hopeless looking for the others.

It had been a very close call for Peter Spear. As he wrote afterwards:

We had heard many avalanches but this one got louder and louder and louder. . . . I looked up through the snow . . . and there was a massive avalanche 50 metres wide and hundreds of feet high coming directly at me. I shouted "avalanche!" at Rusty and tried to dive behind my pack to survive the blast. . . . I was still clipped onto the climbing rope, the wind blast . . . hit me . . . I was hurled and tumbled and bent and bashed by the snow which came cascading over me.

When it stopped, only part of his face and one forearm were clear. He was able to clear his nose and mouth, but was in tremendous pain. His body was pressed in a desperately contorted position, with tremendous tension on the rope at his harness. It was Rusty who found him, after digging himself out, and Rusty and a Sherpa dug him free. Peter felt tremendous relief when the Sherpa slipped a knife down and sliced the rope. His clothes were completely packed with snow, which they quickly beat out, and Rusty supplied a down jacket for the walk back to base. They met the rescue party moving up the ropes.

Peter's diary noted the joy he felt at the sight of them, and they noticed that, as chipper as he seemed to be, he still showed the effects of shock and pain.

OVERLEAF
*Jim Elzinga (left) assisted
by other team members
and Sherpas carry Pasang
Sona's body through the
shattered maze of seracs
and crevasses further down
the icefall.*

Tim related afterwards his feelings as he went down to help with Bill and Dave. "I remember Bill stopping . . . and hollering back to us . . . 'All of the climbers are accounted for,' meaning all of the team members." From further down, though, they heard a shout, "No, we're missing some people." Tim said he knew that when he saw the devastation, the silent, packed field of white, he knew that anybody missing must be dead. He said the realization was ". . . just numbing. It makes your whole body dull."

The men worked quietly, the orders and reports curt and perfunctory, as the shock set in. Tim wrote in his diary:

While digging from the bottom end of the buried fixed rope, a hand was uncovered and the grim reality became clear. It took an eternity to clear the white cement from Pasang's body. . . . James [Blench] asked Bezruchka, "What do we do?"

Bezruchka replied, stifling tears, "We should try CPR (cardio-pulmonary resuscitation). If it was me I would like someone to try."

We put the cold, lifeless body in a sleeping bag with Rusty to try to warm him while Dave McNab and Bezruchka did CPR for almost half an hour. The attempt at resuscitation proved useless and it was obvious that he was dead.

By 9:00 a.m. they realized there was no chance of finding anyone alive, or even of finding other bodies. They decided to bring Pasang Sona's body down. Speedy noted that, as they brought the body down, it was "dark, snowing, and misty" reminiscent of the mood in "a Wagnerian tragedy." Peter Spear wrote that the event was awakening in many the realization that "Everest is not a mountain to be toyed with."

It was a very quiet evening in Base Camp. The final count had been made, so there was no doubt who was where. The body on the stone altar outside was of Pasang Sona. He was 40 years old, from Kunde, and had been on three previous Everest expeditions and on Annapurna I.

Dawa Dorje, one of the two Sherpas whose bodies were not recovered, was also 40. He was from Thame and I knew him well from the winter Annapurna IV expedition. He was a real gentlemen, well dressed, clean cut, and young looking. He had climbed all over in Nepal, and was one of the most experienced Sherpas.

The youngest killed was Ang Tsultim, from Khumjung. He was 20 years old, and this was his first climbing expedition. He had previously worked only with trekking groups.

Climbers and Sherpas bring down Pasang Sona's body across an aluminum ladder spanning a crevasse in the traverse section of the icefall.

Pasang Sona's body, latched to an improvised ladder stretcher, arrives at Base Camp.

After sending messages to the families, writing the official report, and collecting the Sherpas' few belongings, Bill wrote:

It was difficult to sleep that night and I awoke at 1:00 a.m., crawled out of the tent and made my way down to the body. Two Sherpas stood as silent sentinels; it was a beautiful starlit night, with the bright moonlight making the valley like day. A silent prayer was said and I grieved quietly and deeply at the loss we had suffered.

At the same time, in another tent, diary notes of a different tone were being written by Don Serl:

I'm going home. The trip is dead for me and there seems no real reason or cause to revive it. I think we fucked up badly, and that three lives have been spent teaching us a lesson I doubt we can or will learn. We were far too casual about the *other* hazard of the icefall—the avalanches. The seracs and so on proved not to be the problem at all, and diverted our attention from the *real* danger, which none of us recognized in its full scope.

This shortcoming on our part cost those lives, and to say now that "we'll be extremly cautious" is hollow, and probably incorrect, as I believe we *still* don't have the ability to predict this sort of avalanche danger from the shoulder. In fact, it may be really unpredictable, and I'll not willingly walk into that situation now that I realize it exists. . . . And now three Sherpas are dead. . . . I can't accept that . . . my portion of responsibility should include returning to the mountain.

I climb for joy, and challenge and danger too, sure, but there's no way I'll be able to enjoy any more of this trip, and there's too little to life to pass it doing things one doesn't enjoy, at least when one has a choice. So it's away for me. I'm going back to climbing between me and the mountain, where *I* bear the costs, such as they may be, of my errors. Honesty. Directness. Not some horrible situation where three men die and the process can carry on. That's a perversion of any value I care to hold. That's *destination,* not *path,* if ever I saw it. . . .

If, as Rusty suggests, expeditions are emasculating this area, through the deaths of the best and most vital Sherpas, there's a moral question for you. Maybe that in itself justifies self-contained expeditions.

Probably does. Will think about that later, more. Now, to try to get some sleep. May be a bit tough.

OH BARA SAHIB!

FROM THIS LAST DAY of August, from the very beginning of our "official" climbing season, at what was psychologically our most untried, vulnerable period, we faced the unforeseen enemies that lurked around Everest and the high Himalaya. In some ways, yes, these spirits were "of the mountains." But they were not of the mountains most of the Canadians had known up to that point. Every one of us was to learn a great deal—about ourselves, and about the further reaches of the sport to which we were committed.

These enemies were subtle and varied and often appeared as friends— or *other* people's friends. One was the utterly open, ceremonial expression of grief in the traditional Nepalese/Tibetan Buddhist manner. Another was our 1960s style experiments with the same thing, in the more reserved, tentative manner of the "I'm OK—You're OK" school. We tried to believe that to express grief was to share, and that to share was to gain strength. Some of us felt unable to handle this openness, however; we felt ourselves to be demoralized rather than strengthened by it.

Our defense against both these enemies, as it turned out, was essentially old-school stiff-upper-lipism, mixed with some careerist momentum, some opportunism, some determination, some love of the freedom of the hills, and maybe no small dash of national pride.

For most of us, it was the first time we had been expected to take death in our stride and carry on with the operation. That, clearly, was not part of our general idea of sport. It was more like the conditions of war. The Canadian team included a complete range of commitment, daring, fear, shame, pride, and a host of other emotions and character traits that littered that long road from what Rusty, on August 30, called our "bubble of immortality" to the "Vietnam without a rifle" Tim Auger would mention in a midnight radio talk with Kiwi Gallagher two days later. The next seven days were to cut a long, clean line right down the middle of that painful, pulsing mass of intense emotions. I think that, for many reasons, Bill March took that cut right down the middle, and he survived.

Bill and Gyaljen Sirdar (the Sherpa leader) and eight Sherpas who were close to Pasang Sona or to the families of the dead Sherpas, carried Pasang's body. It was wrapped in a Thinsulate sleeping bag, lashed to an aluminum ladder. They worked their way over the glacier rubble, down the steep, dangerous masses of moraine rock. Finally they came to the trail that reaches down, between the field of moraine the glacier has

Bill March, the expedition leader, comforting Pasang Sona's widow at the cremation ceremony.

A relative comforting Pasang Sona's widow at the cremation site.

The offering of prayers and supplications at the cremation ceremony of Pasang Sona. Clouds swirl below, filling the lower Khumbu valley.

pushed out and the mountainside it has been pushed against, to the little dust-coloured collection of stone huts and yak pens that is called Lobuche. Steve Bezruchka and John Amatt, the expedition's business manager, came down soon after.

It was not long after their arrival in the hamlet that they heard the wailing, the heartfelt, traditional crying of Pasang Sona's wife. She was making her way slowly up the road with one of her young daughters. Their faces, as they entered the lodge, wore a flushed, pleading expression that one rarely sees in our Western world, but that here was unleashed, to tear at the hearts of everyone.

Bill went with her into the kitchen of the lodge, where the bound body was being kept, the waxen face a powerful presence in the room. She repeated over and over, "Oh Bara Sahib!" (expedition leader) and said that she wanted to go to sleep with Pasang Sona, that she wanted to die.

Bill and Steve found it devastating to be so close to this small, poorly dressed woman and her dark-eyed little daughter, their eyes red and their faces streaming with tears, their voices expressing the deepest reaches of loss and despair. The men could not understand much of what she said, her voice trembling, her hands shaking, and it was utterly draining to feel in a position of responsibility for Pasang Sona's death, and to be face to face with the result of it.

Bill expressed something about feeling responsible, feeling guilty, and when she totally absolved him, through Gyaljen Sirdar and others as interpreter, Bill felt even more powerfully bound up in the intensity of the woman's grief. She blamed the mountain, saying it was a fateful year, that many were dying in the Khumbu. She did not blame him at all but clung to him for help, and Bill was overcome by a natural feeling of helplessness. He held her, quietly, led through misery by the sounds of her crying, hour after hour.

An older man, walking with a limp and supported by a stick, arrived soon after Pasang Sona's wife. He was introduced as Phu Choton, Ang Tsultim's father. He was a quiet, dignified man, who met Bill with tears in his eyes. Along with other Sherpas who were gathering, he sat, his leathery, wrinkled face glistening with tears, listening to Pasang's wife as though to ritual music, his feelings expressed in her cries. His relative stoicism was just as hard for the Westerners to accept as the women's wailing. Along with Gyaljen Sirdar and a liaison officer from the Ministry of Tourism who had been accompanying the Expedition, Bill and Steve took turns sitting with the mourners, holding them, consoling them.

In the afternoon, a lama arrived from down the valley with a porter and the paraphernalia required for the liturgy of cremation. He joined the grieving, sitting quietly in his robes.

This protracted, exhausting wake eventually brought on a dream-like state, an unreality that Steve and Bill found disorienting, and very, very long. A meal was taken by everyone amid the incessant wailing. The process went on all night long, and was still going on when the sun rose the next morning. Steve and Bill often sat quietly together, each wondering how much of this a person could be expected to take, this ritual unravelling of all one's resources for handling grief.

 COLLAPSE IN THE TRAVERSE

THAT EVENING at Base Camp the weather cleared and the temperature became much colder. As I lay in my tent that night, I could hear, for the first time, heavy cracking from the icefall. The icefall seemed to be moving, and I didn't know if the weather had anything to do with this or not. This crack, groan, crack went on all night. The cracks were caused by pressures in the ice that were being released, tension being released.

In the morning, the group was away by 4:00 a.m. It was a beautiful, clear, cold morning. A perfect day for going through the icefall. James Blench, Dwayne Congdon, Laurie Skreslet, Kiwi Gallagher, Pat Morrow, Jim Elzinga and four Sherpas pushed through to Camp I. The New Zealand expedition was also going to make a carry through the icefall this day. It would be their first carry to Camp I.

Rusty Baillie, Dave Read, cameraman Blair Griffiths, and two Sherpas—Pasang Tenzing and Nima Tshering—went into the traverse in the icefall to refix some of the less stable ladders.

I had eaten breakfast and, with a steaming cup of coffee in my grasp I ducked under the door flap of the kitchen tent. I settled myself on a wicker stool to survey the action in the icefall with a pair of Leica binoculars. The sky was brilliant blue and the sun was beginning to creep down the west shoulder of Everest. It was only 8:30 a.m., but the heat of the sun was already warming my back. The upper section of the icefall was bathed in the sun's rays and I could distinguish small figures moving slowly above the Prow. Another group was moving very quickly downwards. They were the four members of the New Zealand expedition—my brother Adrian, Paul Moores, Peter Hillary, and Fred From—already returning from their first carry to Camp I.

This was one of the first days with really excellent weather we had experienced. The trauma of the avalanche began to evaporate like the thin frost on a sun-warmed rock. I felt confident. People were moving around the camp, beginning their duties of the day. Peter Spear, as always, was at work organizing Sherpa work parties, rebuilding tent platforms, and assembling equipment.

The small figures at the base of the icefall were now getting bigger, and within minutes Peter, Adrian, and Paul came striding into camp. "Heyup youth," Aid called. "Get a brew on. Look comfortable there, don't ya? Surprised you don't have beach chairs. Must be nice, going first class!"

"Yeah. Just finished breakfast: eggs, bacon, and pancakes, you know. Not bad." They strode away, equipment clanking.

I went back to my surveillance. The tiny figures in the upper reaches of the icefall had now disappeared. They must have reached Camp I. I stretched and went to refill my coffee cup. On my way once more to the "sun deck," I noticed Adrian sprinting frantically towards our camp.

"Did you see that, kid?" he gasped. "A whole section of the traverse has just collapsed. Fred just spotted it."

"No." I replied, surprised that I would have missed something so big. "Whereabouts?"

"He said he saw some seracs at the end of the traverse just collapse. All I saw was a kind of mushroom cloud of powder. No sound, just the powder."

We searched with the glasses. It was hard to detect any change in the massive jumble of ice blocks above. But as I searched, the radio crackled into life.

"Rusty to base, Rusty to base. Do you read? Over."

"Base to Rusty. Reading you strength five. Go ahead", I answered.

"There's been a terrible accident in the traverse. I think Blair is dead and maybe also Dave Read and a Sherpa. I repeat, there's been a terrible accident in . . ." Rusty's voice cracked, full of emotion and alarm.

In Base Camp, a group of us assembled quickly to act as a rescue group. The New Zealanders offered to go back up to help with rescue attempts, or to bring down a body, if necessary. I waited for my brother Adrian and we crossed the foot of the icefall together. Slowly we approached the group of people who were descending.

It was the first time on this expedition that I had gone anywhere with Adrian, and I had a real sense of strength and security. This was the first expedition I had ever been on that I hadn't climbed with my brother. Over the last 18 years he had almost always been my climbing partner. When we were walking underneath the Lho La seracs I remember looking up and feeling they wouldn't dare collapse now. I felt more secure climbing with Adrian than with any of the climbers in the Canadian group. This was obviously because he was my brother and because we had climbed a lot together, but also because I knew that Adrian was as strong and determined as I was.

As we started up the fixed ropes Rusty Baillie and Dave Read arrived, visibly shaken. Face to face with them, it became clear that no rescue was needed, but that the situation needed discussion. We decided, in radio consultation with Peter, back at Base Camp, to come back down and work out what we were going to do next.

In camp, Rusty and Dave explained what had happened. They had all been at work repairing a ladder. Blair and Rusty were at the top of the ladder, Dave at the bottom. There were two Sherpas also, one at the top and one at the bottom. There had been a movement, like a small earthquake it seemed, and serac blocks began to collapse around them. Rusty said that he had been standing at the top of the ladder when he saw an ice tower starting to fall towards him. He had realized that if he jumped anywhere he would probably be crushed by other chunks so he just stood there and the tower passed within inches of his face. At the same time, the surface he was standing on began to move. He scrambled to stay on top.

As Dave Read described it later: "The whole glacier started to shudder and shimmy. I thought at first it was an earthquake, but then I realized the entire glacier was moving around me. The piece I was standing on started to slide into the crevasse, and suddenly there were these big blocks of ice all around my head, and I was passing them, and they were going over the top of me, and I thought, 'This is it, mate. Too bad.' "

When the violence stilled, Dave found himself caught at the waist in a jam of rubble at the bottom of a cavern, his feet dangling in loose snow, his head and torso free under a roof of hard ice. Light shone through from somewhere far above. A toque lay near him. He reached for it, and was shocked to realize a head was under it. He was able to a scoop snow away from the face, and suddenly, with a violent cough, the Sherpa came to life, sputtering snow, shouting and struggling. In panic, the Sherpa freed his arms and grabbed Dave to pull himself up. This only pushed the helpless Dave further down, feeling growing desperation as debris gathered around his arms and shoulders.

"My God, you're alive!" Dave suddenly heard. It was Rusty, his face visible in a small hole 20 feet above.

"I won't be for long if this Sherpa has his way!" Dave managed to say, thrashing against the Sherpa and snow.

Rusty lowered a rope. The Sherpa grabbed it, and Rusty took his weight. The Sherpa scrambled up, while Dave dug and cut with a snow stake, knife and ice axe, and finally freed himself from the tangle of rope and ice that held him.

As he made his way up, he asked Rusty how Blair Griffiths was.

"Sorry, Dave," Rusty replied. "He's dead."

Dave climbed over to Blair, whose body was pinned upright between two large slabs of ice.

"He had a very calm look," Dave said later, "as though he was going to talk, to say, 'Hey, you know, I'm only joking.' "

Dave shook Blair's hand, and said, "I'm sorry about that, Blair."

Then he and Rusty began their descent of the new, unfamiliar traverse, following sections of the old fixed rope now stretched far above them.

 ## TRIAL BY FIRE

IN THE VALLEY, Bill March and Steve Bezruchka made their way with the funeral party to a little ridge that led out of the village. Rough stone chorten memorials to other dead stood silently in the clear morning air. There the lama and a couple of assistant Sherpas lifted the body of Pasang Sona out of the Thinsulate bag. They struggled with the weight and with the incipient stiffness of the limbs. The tumbled, tangled pile of wood was already built, on a platform of stone, and they positioned the body in a sitting, or forward leaning, fetal position. Bill and Steve watched in a kind of stupor as the lama cleaned blood, which was oozing out of the mouth, off the face, while his assistants propped pieces of wood around the torso and under the armpits.

Then, the lama held the head up, and in a quiet, solemn manner that, for the Westerners, in no way reduced the grotesque, macabre quality of the act, performed a ritualistic feeding of the body with blessed rice. The widow and Pasang Sona's daughter wailed constantly, and the lama chanted, methodically and thoroughly throwing kerosene over the corpse's skin, until it gleamed with the liquid, and over the gnarled, wood. The smell of kerosene added to Bill's and Steve's growing shock.

By the time a match was touched to the kerosene, and the flames began to lick and sear the flesh, Bill felt he could hardly sort the living Pasang from the dead, and felt that it would have been just as easy to see a living man die, as to see the flames and smoke writhing around the corpse's limbs and face, the grisly, ghastly effect of them on the mouth and eyes and hair. My God! Why couldn't they hide something? The widow was now sobbing uncontrollably, and being held from the flames only by the strength of many people.

It was only when the fire really did begin to consume the corpse that any kind of spiritual significance began to reveal itself to Bill. The act was simple, and it was primitive. But it was also true that the smoke was rising heavenward, that Pasang was now disappearing, physically, and in all other ways. Bill began to feel some of the dignity of death that he had always tried to associate with it in his own culture. That realization allowed the kind of desperate ecstacy that can come from the Western phrase "ashes to ashes." Even though the wailing and the strange harmonies of the chanting continued, Bill at last felt that a spirit, a soul—indeed, a man—was finding fulfillment.

He was. But the grief-contorted face of the widow showed that she was not.

Bill turned from the scene when he realized it was appropriate, and as his own thoughts allowed him to. Just as he did so, a very old, wizened little man in drab woollen garb appeared. The man grabbed Bill's forearm with amazing strength, and his age-paled but intense eyes caught Bill's attention powerfully.

"Let no more Sherpas die!" the old voice said. The eyes looked piercingly into Bill's, searching for a promise. Bill nodded, his feelings scrambling for some kind of validation or honour or strength that would lend conviction to the expression in his own eyes. The old face looked at him another instant, and then turned away, leaving Bill stunned.

"Let no more Sherpas die!"

The order echoed over and over in Bill's mind. He knew it would for a long time. Maybe forever. He felt he could hardly grieve more than he had, but that mystical call to his responsibilities as a leader of human beings was overwhelming.

Bill walked back slowly with Steve and the others toward the buildings of Lobuche. He felt drained and exhausted. He just needed rest. He wanted to get away from the chanting, the smoke, the grisly horror of the burning body, the desperate faces and agonized wails, the loathsome smell of the kerosene and the rhododendron wood, the whole primitive dreamscape. This was not at all what he had imagined this trip would be like. Had he known, he would be back at home with his wife and his children, and his schedule and committees and students, and everthing would be all right. He just needed desperately to get away.

Just then, a Sherpa came up to him, saying he had just arrived from Base Camp. He handed Bill a note. Bill unravelled the twisted, dirty paper. It was Peter Spear's handwriting.

Bill—Very bad news. We had a major collapse in the icefall this morning about 8:30 and Blair Griffiths was killed. Rusty Baillie and Dave Read were near him at work on a bridge when it happened, and they had close calls, but were unhurt. Blair, however, is dead. I'm very sorry. Please give us a radio call when you're free—Peter.

Bill's reaction surprised him. He didn't know whether it was because he was already drained of emotion, or whether it was a suddenly surfacing anger or defensiveness, or whether it was just his training and background, but he received the news very calmly. In his diary, he later noted, "I had no more feeling except a hard, cold pragmatism which I realized was necessary if the expedition was to continue."

Bill immediately called Base Camp. Peter told him they intended to get Blair out and to bring him down to Lobuche for cremation. Bill was aghast at the news. How in God's name could they want to risk still *more* life in the icefall to retrieve a body? And for what reason? To treat the body the way they had just treated Pasang Sona's? He realized that if the whole team were subjected to what he had just been through, they would all quit immediately. It was time to draw the line with a firm hand.

"Negative!" he barked into the radio. "No way will we have more risk of life in the icefall. Leave him!"

There was hesitation on the radio set, and Bill and Steve could hear bits of urgent, incomprehensible discussion.

"Roger, Bill. We acknowledge your feelings. However, there is very strong feeling, I repeat, very strong feeling, that he must be recovered and brought down. Over!"

"Peter, there is no way! I'm not going to stand for it! We have already lost three men in there, now another, and there's just no way!"

There was more hesitation and discussion. Then Peter spoke again: "Roger, Bill. Uh, Bill, I repeat. The feeling here is very strong. I repeat, very, very strong, that the body must be retrieved and brought down— we've got to do it, Bill."

Bill could sense the desperate obstinacy in Peter's voice and in the voices behind him. He couldn't believe the opposition he was getting on a point that was absolutely clear to him. Why take the risk? Why a repeat of horror show? But he felt too exhausted to press the point.

"Roger, Peter. I acknowledge. You feel it's very important. Give me two hours here, to sort some stuff out. I'll call in two hours."

After a moment, Peter's voice said, "Roger. We'll wait your call in two hours. Over. Out."

Bill turned to Steve Bezruchka. Steve speaks with a soft voice, and his warm eyes are framed by the little, metal-rimmed, round-lensed spectacles that were prevalent on university campuses in the sixties. It is a style that I associate with California, and with such concerns as human potential and eastern philosophy.

Bill has been a climbing instructor and guide, and he teaches, among other things, "leadership" at the University of Calgary. He sometimes comes across with the style one might associate with the leader of a British Commando squad. You can easily visualize him in the old war movies, briefing the young RAF Spitfire pilots before a night raid over Germany.

Their long conversation revealed an interesting contrast between the iron leader, on the one hand, and the encounter group therapist on the other. The extremes were modified by mutual respect and mutual need for support in a very trying period. But I think the contrast illustrated a very significant hiatus in the make-up of the Canadian spirit on the expedition.

Bill repeated the stand he had taken on the radio. This was obviously a hard, merciless mountain, and Bill was going to be a hard, merciless leader. It was the only way they stood a chance. If they got Blair out and brought him down for cremation, then everyone on the team would have to go through what Bill and Steve had already been through, which would destroy the morale and motivation of the team.

Steve felt that this was exactly the wrong approach. He said that until the team experienced their tragedy first-hand, by bringing Blair down, and until they expunged their grief, together, in the catharsis of a proper ceremonial expression, they would not be able to find their emotional way back to the reality of climbing the mountain. He felt, furthermore, that it would be impossible to issue orders that would halt their natural impetus to do these things.

What Bill did not know, and Steve perhaps knew or sensed, was that some of the feelings expressed in Don Serl's diary—that it was unthinkable to continue now that men had been killed—were hanging very heavily around Base Camp. I was in the middle of some of these discussions—small groups talking, in an atmosphere of great tension.

Jim Elzinga, an experienced and capable climber, was voicing another aspect of the situation. He felt that the group and its leadership was not adequately tuned in to the realities of the mountain. He, along with two other young climbers, Dave McNab and James Blench, thought that a serious mountaineering error had been made. They knew of the report following the American Medical Research Expedition in 1981 that the particular "valley" we were using in the icefall had been the scene of an avalanche on that expedition too, and had taken out many feet of *their* fixed rope. They knew, from the very appearance of the valley, that it was a well-worn avalanche path.

Offering to the gods after the cremation ceremony.

Further, not only had Bill declined to make or accept a 3:00 a.m. radio call at Camp I on the morning of the avalanche, he had even declined to have Dave McNab, also at Camp I, make one for him. Some felt that this was because Bill had been pushing too hard to be at Camp I, and was using up so much energy on this that he could not make key decisions when they were needed. In other words, he was trying to "lead from the front" instead of from a position of true leadership strength. He had relied on Kiwi Gallagher in Base Camp rather than being there himself. Now the question arose, why didn't *Kiwi* know there was a problem? Why did *he* let the carry go forward?

Of course, it would have been hard for Kiwi to know how much snow there was above. So Bill should have called Base Camp. Or, if Kiwi was unsure, he should have delayed the carry until he could get radio confirmation on conditions at Camp I. Or a more experienced man than Pat Morrow should have been in front with the radio, someone who could take control. Why hadn't they learned from the aborted carry a few days earlier? The questions around Base Camp were many and probing.

I discussed much of this with my brother Adrian and the New Zealanders. We agreed that a three o'clock radio call probably would have saved the Sherpas' lives. But we also agreed that a large expedition produces complex situations, and that it is very easy to second-guess a leader, especially at such an early stage, when everyone is still feeling his way. Everyone needs a *little* luck, especially at the beginning, and right then, the Canadians didn't have enough.

I think that Blair's death did not add any fuel to the questions of technical competence that had been raised. It was agreed that the collapse was, by any conceivable standards, unforseeable. But when Bill came across on the radio as the iron ruler, implying that they should forget about Blair or just bury him in a crevasse, I think some people were wondering if Bill had turned into some kind of monster.

The negative response in Base Camp to his attitude was vehement and spontaneous. Peter's voice on the radio to Bill did not begin to convey the intensity of the resentment. There was no way they were going to throw Blair into a crevasse and forget about him.

Bill may not have been aware that the strong emotions about Blair had in fact built up to the point that an order had come from Kiwi to take down and secure the tents at Camp I, pile them in one place, and cover the lot with a big tarp. This may have been intended merely to secure the

gear for a few days of untended snowfall, until decisions could be made, but to many it seemed to be a statement of finality, representing the true state of their morale at the time. It seemed the tents were being thrown down, the tarps being pulled over everything, for the last time.

THE ROAD TO COLD MOUNTAIN

THAT NIGHT, the ice under Base Camp groaned and creaked and growled, as though unsatisfied and eager for more of us.

We didn't know if the morning's collapse had been a complete shift, or if the whole glacier was still unsettled, in stress, ready for some other section to break under the strain. We wanted to get Blair out but we were fearful of his keeper.

At midnight, unable to sleep because of the noise of the icefall and suspense about the morrow, Tim Auger radioed Kiwi Gallagher at Camp I. He said, "Lloyd, I can't sleep and I'm really scared. I'm going up tomorrow, and it looks like this will be the last thing we do on the mountain. I feel I owe Blair and the climb that much. But I've got to say I don't remember feeling this way before. I feel like I'm in Vietnam and I don't even have a bloody rifle."

At 3:45 a.m. Tim, Don Serl, Dave McNab and I got up and were out at 4:30. The people in Camp I were descending to meet us near the traverse and help us if necessary. The two things on our minds were Blair and the icefall. No one could talk about Blair, so we talked about the icefall. We did what we normally knew to be the worst thing in a scary situation, which was to discuss the hazards and speculate about bad possibilities. I've found this can be just as destructive as its opposite can be constructive: a cheerful, positive attitude can magically dispel fear, especially in a group. But this morning, cheer was far from our emotional reach. Moreover, I knew that Tim was wrestling with some philosophical considerations of fate that were disturbing him.

We agreed that if things began to look too dangerous, we would turn around and come back. That little understanding helped a lot, as we worked up toward the traverse.

Nevertheless, a cold feeling was growing in the pit of my stomach, and it seemed to weaken my legs, even make them feel as though they didn't belong to me any more, not quite under control. Just before the traverse Tim said, "Look, we go in fast, we get the body, we bring him out here and then we can rest and start to take him down. If there is any problem we come back out." I repeated that I fully agreed. Just get in quick, and get out.

I felt better, somehow, once we were actually *into* the traverse, the four of us moving strongly. The danger was there, but at least it was tangible instead of theoretical. It was where I could see it, keep an eye on it. My legs felt stronger. We all looked around, amazed at how such a huge area could be so suddenly and completely changed. At one point we crossed under a huge, balanced tower, squeezing one by one through a small gap. We rushed now, out of breath, and then saw Blair. He was trapped up to his waist, frozen with his left arm held high and sticking out of the ice. Tim rushed up with his ice axe, and with hurried, powerful swings, slashed out showers of the ice that was holding Blair. Don and Dave stood uneasily waiting, since there was only room for one worker.

I climbed up onto some blocks just above the body to get some idea of the damage that had been done to the route, and to assess the safety of going through again. From where I stood, it looked as though there were two huge horizontal fault lines indicating the critical stress points of the main thrust of this section of glacier as it moved over the steepening area. It looked as though the lower section tended to pull away, leaving the upper section hanging until it caught up, with a collapse. Now, the jumble seemed to have packed against the lower fault and looked relatively stable.

I descended when we were ready to move the body. We tied a rope into his harness and, steering the stiff limbs and the crampon points and frozen gear over thousands of obstacles, we rushed, now pushed by the horror of our work more than by danger.

We were panting hard. Many passages were very steep, the bridges were narrow and shaky, the body was heavy and awkward, and we were working very quickly, our nerves stretched thin. We reached the top of a block that felt relatively safe, and wrapped the body in a tarpaulin. It was a merciful advantage having him covered. We finally made safe ground, and from then on it was easier, down the groove made by many feet, back to the bottom of the icefall. The Camp I group had been delayed because they had to make many route repairs just to get through the collapsed section of the upper traverse. Moreover, while working on one ladder, Laurie had fallen some distance, and was in a great deal of pain from what seemed to be a couple of broken ribs.

We all arrived at the foot of the icefall, however, where Speedy and some others met us. We lashed Blair onto a ladder and carried him to Base Camp, where Dave Jones, the doctor, prepared him for transport down to Lobuche.

I went to the chorten at the camp entrance, and sat for a few moments of relaxation. Jim Elzinga came over and asked, "Well, Al, what do you think?" It took me a moment to realize that he was talking about the expedition—whether to stay on—and that he was trying to get a feel for where others stood on this point. I didn't try to form my thoughts to discuss it with him and just shrugged or shook my head. I was going hour by hour, day by day. But leaving was certainly not one of my intentions. For me, there was still a lot more left of this climb.

After lunch, a large number of New Zealanders, Catalans and Canadians streamed off down the valley, taking turns carrying the stretcher. Several of us turned back at Gorak Shep, the little village on the edge of the moraine, and others, who had caught up by then, took over.

The trail was difficult, and Tim kept trying to raise Bill on the radio to ask him to send Sherpas up from Lobuche to help. He couldn't get through, so Tim finally went on ahead. He found Bill in one of the Lobuche tea huts, sitting in the corner and looking very dejected.

Tim said, "Look, we need help, can you send someone back up to help them?" Bill, who normally would stand up and shake hands, just sat there, barely acknowledging his presence.

It was Tim's (in fact, any of the up mountain group's) first direct contact with the situation in Lobuche, and Tim was taken aback. He felt, although he said nothing about it until later, that Bill might have considered Tim a ringleader in the plot to countermand Bill's initial order to leave Blair up there.

I think hindsight reveals that few people had Bill's perspective at the time of the chasm that existed between the idealism of the mountain group and the morbid reality of Lobuche, both heightened by shock. Bill, at least, could imagine from past experience what was going on up the mountain. Most of the team members, however, had nothing in their experience to prepare them for what awaited them in Lobuche.

Long ago, protective symbols resembled the threats they were meant to guard against. The viking ships had sea monsters on their prows; the enduring symbol for medicine has been a snake, feared from the beginning of time. I think Bill was hardening into a symbol of Everest. He was determined to hold fast, to do just what the mountain was doing, which was to hammer out a team that could make it.

In Bill's mind (and I can only speculate) "team" seemed to signify a progressive melding of himself and the 16 climbers under his command into one steely resolve: to get at least one of them, whichever one was in place and in good shape at the right time in the right conditions, to the summit.

The mountain though, is bigger than Bill and bigger than any man, and it spoke more subtly and more profoundly than Bill realized. First, the mountain reminded some climbers that, in addition to faces and buttresses and a summit, the mountain also claimed as its domain this strange mystical culture through which the Westerners were walking as if in a dream. It was demanding that each man envision his own soul going up in rhododendron smoke, and that each man choose Everest as his first and last, be prepared even to *be* chosen by the mountain.

I can only speculate about what happened that evening in Lobuche. All the team members seemed numbed by the events of the day and the foretaste of the morrow.

In one sense, nothing happened. Many men were simply plodding minute by minute, feeling exhausted and unsure of themselves, and in no way ready to come to grips with their doubts. In another sense, though, a negative momentum was developing. There were feelings of alienation. The bright National Team self-image was cracking. This period, in hindsight, seems littered with inconclusive shreds of evidence and opinion regarding where people stood, what they felt.

Soon after the stretcher bearers arrived, Bill invited Jim Elzinga outside for a talk. He asked Jim what he thought. The two men afterwards gave far different accounts of the conversation that ensued.

Jim said he confided to Bill that he was wondering whether the climb was worth it, and said he was thinking about leaving. According to Jim, Bill then launched into a series of insults and accusations. He said that Jim "cared too much about people, about the Sherpas." He said that Jim was a threat to his leadership. He compared Jim's attitude to mine, saying that whereas I was steadfastly positive, Jim and others were wallowing in unproductive pity. Jim was completely alienated by this exchange.

Bill maintained afterward that Jim misunderstood this whole conversation. He said that he was simply trying to get Jim to drop inappropriate sympathy, to rise above his grief, and to keep his own self-respect and identity as a climber. Only in this way could he get on with tackling what was obviously a very tough mountain.

After talking with Jim, Bill asked Tim outside for a chat. Bill put his arm on Tim's shoulder, and they walked across the meadow as they talked.

Tim recalled later that he opened the conversation with an icebreaker along the lines of "We've sure had a spell of tough events, eh?"

Bill's reply took Tim completely by surprise. He said, "I think I know where you're at, Tim. You've got a wife and little kid at home. I think you should leave. I certainly wouldn't mind."

Tim hadn't seen Bill since before the avalanche, back when everything was gung ho. He struggled to adjust to this change in attitude. What had changed Bill so much? Tim also reeled under what seemed an almost planned attack on his weakest point. Tim *had* been wavering, but was struggling to keep himself together, and the last thing he needed right now was to be, in effect, invited to leave.

Bill went on to say that he understood that when Tim had the decision to make about whether to leave Blair in a crevasse, or to do the "human thing" and bring him down for a funeral, Tim had decided to do the "human thing."

Tim hadn't seen himself as the decision-maker at all; yet he felt he was being pinpointed as the ringleader in countermanding Bill's wishes.

Bill went on to say that this mountain would need hard people. This left the powerful impression in Tim's mind that Bill meant that Tim wasn't one of them, didn't have the "right stuff." Thus, a second man was left feeling quite alienated by his conversation with Bill.

Other climbers seemed to want to discuss things with Bill. Because there were some western trekkers in the hut, and also some Sherpas who understood English, the locale was not conducive to frank group discussion, and feelings remained unformed and unexpressed.

Bill, on the other hand, later claimed that a meeting had in fact taken place in the hut. It seems true that the team had dinner together, but many did not see that as a true meeting, and certainly did not open themselves in discussion.

Whatever actually happened, it seems clear that the rift was growing, and that the evening in Lobuche was a critical turning point in the Expedition's fortunes.

On the morning of September 4, Blair Griffiths' body was taken down the valley to a small point of flowered ridge called Dugla, where chortens stood like spirits in the cold mist and ground clouds that swirled around the quiet throng of climbers and Sherpas. Many of the men wept openly as they committed their friend to the gnarled, twisted wood.

Blair was a quiet man, calmly self-assured. The evening before his death, I'd discussed with him various principles involved in producing the film of the climb he was working on. I'd said that I felt that the film should be a true story, not a news spectacular, and he agreed. I had realized from that discussion and from the way he worked that in addition to being a very able climber, he was an artist.

On the trek in, at Pangboche monastery, he had spent an afternoon gazing at the mountains towards Ama Dablam, and looking down over the tree-covered valley below. He'd written in his journal, "I don't want to die, but if the pale horse should decide to come along there isn't a better cathedral to stay in."

Bill asked the group if members would like to say a few words, Quaker-style, as the pyre was lit. Each in turn stepped forward.

Bruce Patterson, the news correspondent, saluted Blair as a journalist: "You were willing to risk your life . . . you join a long list of distinguished people."

Dave McNab said that "a little bit of us goes with you, and a little bit of you stays with us. Thanks for that."

Tim Auger had composed a poem:

This is the way of all eternity:
As we see him now, so shall we be.
When the time comes to follow him
Where the mountain wind blows,
Go as he does, with a good heart.

Rusty read from a Chinese poem:

I climb the road to cold mountain
The road to cold mountain never ends.

Rusty Baillie and Steve Bezruchka stayed behind to make sure everything was completed with respect and dignity.

PARTINGS

IN SPITE of the horror and fear of the past five days, and even though many of the men felt they had been pushed to their limits, there was much more to come: more hurt, and more anger, and both were going to run very deep.

By the time the men were wandering back up the moraine toward Base Camp, some alone with their thoughts, some in quiet, personal discussion with friends, others in heated arguments, Jim Elzinga had already ordered six yaks to go up to Base Camp the next day to haul down gear. He, James Blench, and Dave McNab had already decided to leave.

The next day was very tense. Anger was surfacing, some of it open, seeking allies, some of it sullen and vengeful. Jim Elzinga was by now convinced that Bill March had been so influenced by the spectre of sponsors and public opinion and his career and a host of other superficialities that he was expecting the group to proceed with blinders on, and was in no way willing to face the possibility that errors had been made in judgement and procedures which, unexamined, could kill more people. He and his young friends James Blench and Dave McNab expressed these views vehemently to other members of the group.

Their questioning seemed to have started out openly and innocently, but as Bill went into his tent and did not come out to discuss the matter, the tone became increasingly harsh and accusatory. The subject of "the three o'clock radio call" the night before the avalanche was raised again. What was Bill to do, presented with what started out as a concern to be shared, but became, as the day wore on and Bill remained aloof, more and more bitter, and ended as an accusation? If Bill acknowledged that new procedures were needed, then he would be admitting error, and would also be giving credit to men he was beginning to perceive as adversaries.

I knew that Bill's horrors went beyond what Jim and the other two imagined. Bill was the leader. He was responsible, in his own mind, for the lives on the expedition. Even worse, perhaps, were his memories of participation in the Royal Air Force Dhaulagiri IV climb, in 1974. The team took a shortcut up the middle of a snow gulley, which he was opposed to, and three Sherpas were killed in an avalanche. Even on the Everest training climb to Nuptse, on which he was deputy leader in 1981, an avalanche scored a direct hit on the advance Base Camp, destroying and burying it, fortunately with no one in it.

And now, he had heard that terrifying roar yet again, and had helped to dig out Pasang Sona's cold, stiff body, and had endured those draining hours with Pasang's wife and the other villagers, and had lead the men through the poignantly personal and sad cremation of Blair. . . .Now, he was living with his own doubts. It was too much to have people pointing fingers at him.

Tim and Rusty discussed with others the possibility that the expedition should shut down. This angered some members. I felt that, as the day wore on, the group was not far from using its fists — or worse. I confess I was glad to have the outlet of the New Zealand camp, where I could talk with Aid in relative tranquility. It gave me much-needed perspective. But I also was at least something of a sounding board for some of the other men of the Canadian expedition. I was not completely candid with them, however. I confess I was motivated by considerations that I don't think had occurred to many of the others.

One factor was that there was a world of difference between the Polish Pillar (or the Canadian Spur) and such alternatives as the American Medical Expedition Route or the standard South Col route. For such alternative routes, we had actually been member-heavy to start with.

Another consideration was that there were already 120 loads of supplies above the icefall. The loads had been assembled, as usual, to provide a cross-section of supplies, so that if deliveries had to stop at any time, for whatever reason, no vital ingredients would be missing for the camp occupants. Even without any more carries, a *small* team could climb the mountain, by an easier route. So when it came to loyalty to team members versus loyalty to the summit, my summit loyalty had me calculating possible departures against that supply base at Camp I.

Another observation of mine was that 16 climbers and 30 Sherpas have (assuming strong members) quite a lot of drive and staying power. But 30 Sherpas and ten, six, or even two climbing members could have even more, especially with powerful lead climbers. And, as I had always maintained, I preferred small expeditions.

My only moral bind was that many of the climbers were using me as a sounding board for their own decision-making. When someone asked me what my intentions were, I might, had I been more calculating, have said, "Are you kidding? I'm getting off this ship before she goes down with all hands!" I didn't say anything like that; on the other hand, I did not reveal my strong commitment to the climb, and simply said that I hadn't made up my mind.

Some speculated that Bill was just waiting for a solid excuse to cancel the climb. It seems to me that he was divided, and that he made no secret of it. In a long conversation with Steve, he had said that part of him would like nothing better than to go home to his family, but that "the mountaineering part" of him could see no reason not to continue with the climb.

His choice may have been reinforced, perhaps unconsciously, by a realization similar to mine, that he could end up with a lightweight group of more committed climbers, and a more attainable objective. He wrote in his notes, "I asked the team members who were leaving to leave as soon as possible, since I felt it would be bad for morale to have them in Base Camp." There was the other side of the coin, however: "The team members who were pondering the decision I gave all the time in the world to and asked them to stay at Base Camp."

Don Serl, as the diary quoted earlier shows, had made up his mind after the Sherpas' deaths to leave. His decision was reinforced by grief for Blair, who had been his friend. Although Don had done a great deal of climbing in the Coast Ranges, Alaska, Peru and with Speedy on Annapurna IV, I suspect, too, that he realized Everest was just more mountain then he wanted to deal with.

Rusty's case was different. He had noted frankly, in his diary, that, yes, because Everest was Everest, he was willing to take more risk on it than he would on another mountain of less fame and stature. But he also pointed out that the Khumbu Icefall is an objective hazard you would never accept on any other mountain. Rusty went in with his eyes open, and watched the debt grow. The first avalanche nearly buried him. Then, in the icefall collapse, he narrowly escaped Blair's fate, when a falling serac missed him by inches.

Bill said afterwards, perhaps seriously, that if Rusty hadn't resigned, Bill would have sent him home anyway. There was something very ominous about so many close calls, so much involvement. I think Rusty was able to evaluate, in a very reasoned way, just how much stress he needed in his mountaineering career at this point, and decided it was time to draw the line.

Tim Auger was one of the first to talk with Bill about leaving, the first to get the "that's fine, please make it quick" message. Tim seems to have a sense of wonder about him, so that perhaps strict objectivity is not always the main point for him. In evaluating the amount of snow it should take to make the icefall unsafe, for instance, he mused, "How many snowflakes is too many?" Such a tangent perhaps illustrates items of faith he had not been able to resolve.

On a previous expedition, Tim had met a Sherpa Sirdar who had been born in the same year. This fact was interesting to the Sherpa, and he shared with Tim an intricate horoscope that the Sherpa knew would apply to both of them. The Sherpa pointed out to Tim that they would have many ups and downs, but that the Year of the Water Dog, 1982, was definitely a year to avoid danger, and specifically, big mountains. That sincere and confident prediction had been in the back of Tim's mind throughout the planning and the start-up of the Canadian expedition. Its pessimism began to blend logically with the fate that seemed to be unravelling right here and now. By the time we were on our way to get Blair out, Tim believed that he probably would not live much longer on this expedition.

Tim was also deeply committed to his family, and was always conscious that they were worrying about him every day that he was on the climb, and he felt sad about that. I was very sad to see Tim go, because I had been climbing with him above Camp I and I was looking for a summit partner. Tim, strong and easy-going, had seemed the most likely of the rest of the climbers.

Laurie Skreslet and Dave McNab also went to ask Bill to have a talk. He told them what he had told Tim—that if they were going, they should leave quickly. Jim then went to Peter Spear, to see if Peter would persuade Bill to talk with them. Jim Elzinga said he heard Bill shouting at Peter, but the meeting was set up. Laurie, Dave, James Blench, Jim, and Peter got together with Bill. Dwayne Congdon came in a little later.

The meeting achieved nothing, and lines simply hardened. But there was never one precise scalpel incision that left two cleanly severed teams, one marching down valley in unison, the other setting out arm-in-arm to climb the mountain. For instance, Dwayne Congdon, who ended up performing superbly on the climb, wrote of his feelings at this point: "I was dismayed that some people were still so committed to the climb. I didn't know how they had the guts to continue. I think I was simply scared for myself at this stage."

In fact, Dwayne sent his gear down with the yaks, and was only staying in Base Camp because he knew that his girlfriend was either in Kathmandu or on her way up towards Base Camp. He wanted to reach her by radio to arrange for her to wait, so that she wouldn't get all the way up there and find him gone. As he waited (and as she finally showed up in Base Camp with no radio contact), and as he began to sense the momentum developing in camp, he began to have second thoughts. He decided to stay around and see what happened, taking advantage of Bill's condition that as long as you were thinking of staying on board, you could sit and think.

Laurie Skreslet was immobilized with his broken ribs. Yet, at one point he told me, "If you stay, I will."

Kiwi Gallagher, too, was still undecided. He wrote in his diary, "I was wondering within myself if I should continue with the climb. Thinking of my family, I wondered if the risk was too high for me to carry on."

On September 5, Dave McNab and Tim Auger left with four yaks carrying their own gear and that of Jim Elzinga, James Blench, Rusty Baillie, Dwayne Congdon and Don Serl. Except for Dwayne, the owners of this gear left the next day with six porters.

WE'RE RIGHT BEHIND YOU

THE FOUR WERE TO LEAVE early in the morning on September 6. Dave Jones, the 50-year-old Base Camp doctor, who had not been involved in the arguments and the upsets, had for some days been coming to the realization that his body was not acclimatizing properly to the altitude at Base Camp. He decided he'd better take advantage of the others' accompaniment to go down to lower altitude before he suffered serious damage. That made a total of seven fewer people on the expedition. At this point, one conceivably could have argued that the most unified part of the team was the six who were walking down the trail.

The truly disparate personalities who remained now confronted each other in the Base Camp cook tent. The questions to be answered were: whether to continue the climb, and if so, how and by what route. A long, rambling discussion took place there, chaired by Bill. Outwardly, he was open to suggestions, but positions gradually polarized. I found that each time I mentioned a positive solution, Bill would acknowledge it, and then by some unconscious twist of logic, would sum up the point by saying: "We have an option to quit, as well. Let's just call it a day, you know?" or ". . . we will abort the expedition. We can do that." or "I'm prepared to stack it and go home."

Bill continued in this vein, saying the Sherpas were demoralized, that manpower was reduced, that co-operation with the New Zealanders was inappropriate, that morale was low, and that it just didn't make sense to continue. However, at one point, he began writing options, as suggested by the group, on his clipboard. This seemed to provide some kind of impetus, and he finally said, "I'm prepared to stick it out right to the end of October, just hang in there . . . and then eventually get someone on Everest just by sheer tenacity. If you want that. . . ."

Gradually, some kind of consensus developed to go ahead and climb the mountain. The preferred route was the standard South Col route, which raised the question of co-operating with the New Zealanders.

The essence of the problem was that, if we decided to take the South Col route on Everest, we would be using the same route for much of the way that the New Zealanders would use to climb Lhotse, because the two mountains are linked at the South Col. We were, in spite of our losses, still a heavyweight, high-powered operation. The New Zealanders' aim, on the other hand, was to climb Lhotse lightweight style. It would seriously compromise their ethic if trail were already broken, camps were in place, and ropes were fixed on their route. (One could hardly expect that, to preserve their ethic, they would avoid stepping in our tracks, climb five feet to the side of our path, stay out of our tents, or fix a *second* rope right alongside ours. Their ethic would be erased by ridiculousness.)

By mid-afternoon, I had reached the point where I had had enough of all the discussion, and wandered over to the New Zealand camp. I looked forward to their perspective and their chang. We passed an hour or two talking. As dinner time drew near, I went back to the Canadian dining tent.

In the meantime, John Amatt, our business manager, had come up from Namche Bazaar, where he had been radioing reassurance to the climbers' families after the avalanche. He had encountered all of the departing climbers on the trail and learned of the split in the team. When I entered the dining tent, Bill and John were deep in discussion, neither of them looking as though he were enjoying it. I stood near them for a moment, getting the drift.

John was saying that, in his view, it was vital to cancel the expedition as a whole, otherwise the sponsors and the media would consider it a humiliating rout. He said that the media would catch Rusty and Jim and the others down valley and explode the whole thing out of all proportion. The only answer was to unify behind an orderly retreat, prepare a dignified story about how the deaths were the reason the expedition was being discontinued, and also get to the team members who had left and brief them before they embarrassed everyone concerned.

I realized in an instant that it looked as if Bill might be agreeing with him! I quickly looked around the tent; I saw Speedy and many others. I felt my anger rise like heat from somewhere deep right up into my head, and explode. I shouted. The essence of what I said was that I had for Christ's sake had enough. I had had enough of whether to stay, whether to go, whether to climb, whether to retreat, whether to go on some hero route, whether to join the Lhotse group. I said it was bloody well time to turn this mess into a climb and get on with it. I said that if Bill and John and anybody else were looking for a cop-out, why didn't they just get some yaks up, throw their baggage on, and take off like the others.

The more I said, the more I needed to say and could say. I added that I didn't care how many left—the more deadwood we got rid of, the better —because their leaving took absolutely nothing from me, from *my* Everest trip. But if they wanted to cancel the whole expedition, then they *were* taking something away that was mine, and I wasn't going to stand for it. I noticed at one point in my tirade that the room was quite silent, although many wore interested expressions.

I continued that if Bill or John or any of them were afraid of continuing they should simply say so truthfully, rather than trying to cover their own cowardice by rationalizations about orderly retreat or Air Canada or public image. Just speak the truth so that the rest of us could get on with the climb.

After a short silence, Bill said, "Yes, Al. But I must think of my family."

I was furious. He was unconsciously acknowledging my own point, that if he was afraid for himself or his family, he could say so, but this was not a justification for taking ten other guys down the valley with him. He and John looked at each other and then looked around the room. I sensed that they might actually be winning. There might actually be a cancellation. It was time for my trump card. My last chance.

"If you pack this expedition in," I said, "I'm going to wait until the last yak leaves Base Camp. Then I'm going to the Lhotse camp. We'll get radio permission to climb Everest in your place, and we'll move right up to Camp I, provision for the route with the gear that's there, and we'll carry on. We'll get Canadians on the top in spite of you."

The silence in the room was impressive. John and Bill wore the expressions of men caught in a dilemma.

It was quiet during dinner. Afterwards, John said, "Look guys, it's your lives. If you want to go on with the climb, and you think you can do it, then I'll do whatever I can to help it happen. But as far as I'm concerned, I don't think I'm going back on the mountain again."

I was still angry, and the question that crossed my mind was, "Yeah, you and a lot of others will be right behind us. What I want to know is, how *far* behind?"

Speedy came up to me, and repeated what I already knew—that he was with me. That felt very good. Speedy really showed his strength in crises like this, and I knew that I could rely one hundred percent on him. He may not have been the strongest of climbers on the mountain, but he was certainly one of the most tenacious. No one else had much to say about my tirade. I think they were just waiting to see which way the wind would blow.

Nothing was resolved that evening. Nima Tenzing, a Sherpa from Pangboche who had been on Dhaulagiri with me, had sent his daughter up to Base Camp with five gallons of chang. A few of us went over to the Sherpa tent to share the chang and build some bridges.

The Sherpas were all very nervous about the expedition. The Sirdar, Gyaljen, mentioned that this was his seventh expedition, and that, since seven was an unlucky number for him, he didn't want to continue. (He never went through the icefall again.) Nawang Karma, the Deputy Sirdar, also felt apprehensive about going through the icefall again. Gyaljen was actively trying to persuade him and the other Sherpas not to continue.

It's traditional that, at the end of an expedition, all the equipment and food that is left over is sold to the local people. The Sherpas have first choice and the person with the most authority in the buying and selling is the Sirdar. In other words, he has a vested interest. If the expedition finishes early, he stands to gain more. I suspected this might be a factor in trying to persuade the Sherpas not to continue. Losing their support would certainly undermine the strength of this expedition.

It was time for a sales pitch. I appealed to the Sherpas I knew from other expeditions, reminding them of how good my brother and I had been to work with, and reminding them of their own belief that *zongly* (twins) have much better than average luck. I told them that from now on, the expedition was going to change. The bad karma of the old expedition had disappeared with the men who had left, and this was now a different expedition: this expedition had good karma. I said that if anyone wished to stay in Base Camp, that was OK, but if they felt lucky, felt that they had good karma, I would like them to come with me.

Whether all this reduced the tension, I don't know. At least the five gallons of chang relaxed the atmosphere. In fact, after some time, as laughter and conversation became more prevalent, I began to detect something I hadn't thought of until that moment (and maybe the Sherpas hadn't either). This was that they might be starting to look upon their new situation as a repeat of the Korean climb, in which there had been so many Sherpas compared to Koreans that it was almost a Sherpa climb.

Now they were once again discussing doing the American Medical Research Expedition route, their confidence high, even though I mentioned some of the challenges involved. These didn't deter them. I then asked which of them was prepared to lead on the steep ice. But they laughed, and joked, and avoided answering directly. By the time we left the Sherpa tent, however, I felt that we could get their support.

The following morning, September 7, we awoke to the thunder of crashing rocks and debris falling down from the Lho La. The 300-foot corner that I remembered climbing in the winter of 1980–1981 had fallen off. Thousands and thousands of tons of rock came crashing down the route from the Lho La, taking away much of the Catalan fixed rope. The mountain seemed determined to remind us of its dangers.

Nevertheless, many of the climbers now said they were prepared to continue with the climb. I think they had considered the alternatives. At the moment it was possible to pay lip service to continuing, but I was interested to see how they would hold up when the work really started.

 SOME KIND OF COMPROMISE

WE HAD JOKINGLY designated ourselves CRASS —Canadian Remnants Attempt on Sagarmatha's Summit— "Sagarmatha" being the Nepalese name for Everest. Now that this group was more or less in place, the question arose, what to do with it?

(Things were moving fast around there. We hadn't been on the expedition a month yet, and already we were getting down to brass tacks about what to climb!)

As this was, first and foremost, a *Canadian* venture, it seemed fitting that we should start out with some kind of compromise. The Canadian Spur was obviously beyond our present capabilities, but both the South Col and the American Medical Research Expedition route were still options. Bill and others were attracted to the AMRE route, largely because it avoided the problems of working with the New Zealand team. The Sherpas were rather in favour of the AMRE route as well, on the grounds that no one had ever been killed on it, and because there was an avalanche hazard on the Lhotse face. (It was useless to point out that people had been climbing the South Col route for nearly 30 years, while the AMRE route had been climbed only once, thereby creating something of a statistical anomaly.) The Sherpas did not point out, but I suspect they were thinking, that it is easier to do any route with one boss than it is with two, as they were afraid would be the case if we combined with the New Zealanders.

I, however, felt that our team, as it was, could not succeed on the AMRE route. I thought that it was worthwhile risking the icefall again for a good summit prospect, but not for certain failure on the AMRE route. Bill's diary noted, "I favoured the AMRE route, which would avoid us asking the Lhotse team for permission; however, Alan vetoed this, saying he would not take part in an attempt on that route and favoured the South Col."

The main point for me was that we had one or perhaps two, at most, leaders who could lead through the steep ice at altitude on the AMRE route. On the South Col route, we had a few more members, and certainly one or two Sherpas who already knew the difficulties and could lead through them.

Another factor was that, traditionally, lightweight expeditions use the fixed, bridged route of concurrent heavyweight expeditions through the Khumbu Icefall. The New Zealanders had been planning to do this with the Canadian expedition, realizing that the Canadians would probably take as long to climb the Canadian Spur as it would take the four New Zealanders to climb Lhotse. In this way, the New Zealanders would have a route back out through the icefall after they had completed their climb.

Now, with much less gear to haul and a simplified objective, but still with the power provided by the Sherpas, it was conceivable that the Canadians could be up and down much faster than the New Zealanders. The latter might then confront, after the exhaustion and depletion of a hard route, the prospect of somehow making it through the icefall with nothing but bits of broken rope and aluminum where the Canadian highway had once been. That gave us a nice bargaining point.

It must be noted, however, that long before either expedition left home, the New Zealanders had offered to help the Canadians fix the icefall, as a gesture of goodwill. The Canadian Mount Everest Society had refused to have the proposed Canadian achievement sullied by anything of the sort. This little rebuff was still remembered in the other camp.

The New Zealanders' strongest bargaining point was that it was *they* who had permission to climb Lhotse, not us. And the South Col route has to use about one vertical mile of the Lhotse face. Any Canadian application to interfere with their route could easily be vetoed by them.

The two teams' Nepalese liaison officers were at least as panicked about these factors as the English speakers were, no doubt visualizing the yards of bureaucratic red tape they would have to cut through.

After much discussion among ourselves, we got together with the New Zealanders for what one might optimistically call a "summit" meeting. After some hours of intense discussion, agreement was reached on a rather complex arrangement. It was agreed that the two teams would retain their separate identities: New Zealanders and Canadians. They would, however, climb together up to a point just below the South Col. There the New Zealanders would branch off right toward the summit of Lhotse and the Canadians would branch off left toward Everest's South Col. (John Amatt's concern that Air Canada might not wish to mix New Zealanders and Canadians was overcome by force of numbers).

The New Zealanders could use our food and equipment at Camp I so that they could immediately start fixing rope up the Lhotse face. The New Zealanders also had the right to exclusive use of the Lhotse face until they had evacuated and moved beyond Camp III, or until September 30, whichever came first. This was drawn up in writing and signed by Bill March and Peter Hillary. The signing produced a good, optimistic feeling, and for the first time in many days, an air of happiness moved through the tents of that high, remote valley.

It was agreed in our group that when the helicopter came into Base Camp the next day to do television interviews, John Amatt would go out on it, to take up position in Kathmandu as media liaison officer. We were becoming aware that, what with the accidents, various members walking off, and our decision to climb a different route with a bunch of foreigners, the media might have a few questions.

The next day, Claude Taylor, President and Chief Executive Officer of Air Canada, who had been keeping tab on events, wrote us a letter:

September 8, 1982

Mr. Bill March
Leader
Canadian Mount Everest Expedition
Base Camp
Mount Everest

Dear Bill:

With sincere appreciation for the tremendous challenges and decision you are facing at this time, I would like to assure you of my personal support, and that of Air Canada, for whatever course of action the expedition pursues.

Yours sincerely,

Claude I. Taylor

Some days later, when he received this letter, Bill answered:

September 19, 1982

Dear Claude Taylor:

Many thanks for your letter of support, it was very much appreciated by all the team members who are continuing with the climb. The past few weeks have been extremely difficult for me both as a climber and as a leader. However, I am absolutely convinced that the expedition should continue, albeit with a changed objective in view of the loss of 6 climbing members. The remaining members are 100% behind me and given some good weather I sincerely believe we have a chance to place a Canadian on the summit.

At the present time Camp I is established at 19,600 feet and we have ferried over 30 loads to Camp II at 21,400 feet. We will be establishing two further camps, III and IV, the latter on the South Col at 26,000 feet. From there we hope to make one push for the summit, using oxygen. You will no doubt hear of our progress through the media.

I just want to stress to you that what we are doing is for our own personal reasons, not for the media and not for Air Canada. We are all climbers here and our love and commitment is to climbing — we are grateful for Air Canada giving us the opportunity to attempt Everest. However, everything above Base Camp is a mountaineering decision and always will be.

Perhaps I could end on a quote which I feel is particularly appropriate for this situation: "It matters not whether you win or lose, but how you play the game". The remaining team members and myself are still playing the game.

Yours sincerely,

Bill March
Leader
Canadian Mount Everest Expedition, 1982

Things were looking a lot better all around.

TILMAN TRIUMPHANT

THE INITIAL PLAN was that Bill, Pat Morrow, Speedy Smith, and I would go first, breaking trail through the icefall again. The following day eight Sherpas would join us, carrying loads, and they would begin to push all the loads from Camp I up towards Camp II.

Kiwi Gallagher was complaining of a bad back and was going to wait at Base Camp. Dave Read was also suffering from a bad back and was further demoralized because he hadn't received any letters from his girlfriend, so he also decided to stay at Base Camp. Laurie Skreslet, whose ribs were damaged, still seemed enthusiastic to continue but decided to wait and see what happened in the icefall. Dwayne remained undecided about whether he was staying or not. John Amatt would be leaving to be our public relations man, dealing with the press in Kathmandu. So at this point there were only four people who were prepared to go back up to Camp I.

On September 8, the helicopter eventually arrived. After a rather heavy landing on the small, square landing pad we had constructed, it deposited one television reporter who was obviously suffering from the altitude. He set up his video equipment and proceeded to do an interview with Bill March. It amused me that when the media arrived, an amazing number of expedition members abandoned their lethargy to be present.

That afternoon, Speedy and I sat down and worked out the logistics of the final ascent. It took us about 10 minutes on one sheet of paper (the "back of the old envelope—" Tilman triumphant!). We had projected that, with Sherpa support, and allowing for bad weather and fatigue, and the fact that most of the team wouldn't be performing very well, we could reach the summit within 30 days of leaving Base Camp.

MOUNT EVEREST
Canadian Expedition Route 1982

1. icefall collapse
2. avalanche site
3. Camp I
4. Western Cwm
5. west flank of Nuptse
6. Camp II
7. Camp III
8. Camp IV
9. fracture line of the fatal avalanche
10. west shoulder of Nuptse
11. Lhotse
12. Camp II
13. Camp III
14. Lhotse face
15. Geneva Spur
16. attempted New Zealand route on Lhotse face
17. South Col — Camp IV
18. summit ridge
19. southwest face
20. west ridge
21. north ridge (Tibet)
22. proposed South Spur route

By September 9, it appeared that the lead team of four people would be reduced to three. Bill March had decided that he was going to go down to Namche Bazaar. He had one or two things he said he could do while he was down there; for example, he wanted to get some new charms for the Sherpas from the Lama in the Pangboche Monastery. But everyone realized that he was going down to sort out his own emotional problems before returning to the mountain.

It had been snowing most mornings and afternoons, and there was a lot of wind higher up. It was much colder now during the day, and I was quite adamant that we wouldn't go back up through the icefall until there had been at least two days of good weather to lessen the avalanche threat. People were constantly harrassing me: "When will it be time to go, how will we know?"

All I could think of to say was, "When the weather clears, you'll know—it'll be obvious."

On the morning of Friday, September 10, Speedy Smith, Pat Morrow, and I finally left for Camp I, followed one hour later by the four New Zealanders. Finding the trail was difficult, because no one had gone up towards Camp I for more than 10 days. When we eventually located the beginning of the fixed rope, we found that the snow had melted during the day and refrozen at night, creating a thick crust through which the rope had to be pulled. The rope was two feet under the snow. It required heave after back-wrenching heave to extricate it.

Speedy carried some of my load while I broke trail. It was really exhausting work, and at one point I asked Pat Morrow to break trail. After about 150 feet he stopped and gave it up. Pat always seemed able to get himself where he wanted to go on the mountain, but he wasn't really strong enough to fix rope or carry heavy loads, and I was somewhat skeptical as to what use he would be toward the expedition's objectives. It's one thing to have someone who can lead and support his own weight, and quite another to have someone who can manage to get himself there but is totally dependent on support from either Sherpas or other Westerners.

As I broke trail that morning, I was glad to be in action again. All the frustration of waiting in Base Camp was released as I pushed at the jumars, tearing the rope out of the snow. I found a great deal of satisfaction in doing that. Gradually daylight arrived, and I could see the four New Zealanders catching up with us. They were carrying quite heavy loads, and one of them offered to come in front to break trail. But I would look back from pulling the ropes and see Adrian smiling up at me, occasionally throwing out a challenging or encouraging comment: "Well done lad, keep it going." It was great to have someone behind me who understood and appreciated the work.

At last we came in sight of the big serac marking the beginning of the traverse—the hazardous section. It had been relatively safe up to now. There were some ice towers hanging above us but they seemed reasonably safe and I didn't feel there was any real danger.

It had already started to snow and it was obvious, looking down the valley towards the south and southwest, that snow clouds were blowing in. They were quickly filling the valley around Base Camp and gradually rising up toward our altitude of around 18,000 feet. My confident statement, "You'll know when the weather is good" was starting to seem a little hollow.

We dug a place, dumped our loads, and I shot some video tape of Speedy moving into the traverse. No one else fancied going into it. They started back, while I stood at the entrance and watched Speedy go 150 yards in, pulling the ropes free. I shouted, "Ok, Speedy, come on back. Let's get out of here!" He rejoined me and we started down. On the way we found and reset many of the marker wands that would lead us through the dark to snow-covered ropes on subsequent mornings.

For the next three days the weather was mediocre to bad, snowing most of the day and clearing a little at night. The Catalans had a big party on September 11, and invited us over to get drunk with them. They had an incredible spread of food—we really appreciated the salami, ham, and tinned quail.

Peter Spear brought over an armload of bottles of rum and vodka, donating it to the spirit of the enterprise. As everyone loosened up, we were all slapping one another on the backs and singing. Somehow a table broke and became the garbage crevasse for used cutlery and utensils. My foggy vision of Adrian looming over it with a large knife in his hand suggested to me that this was an appropriate moment for departure. In a quick couple of steps I disarmed him, and then I ushered him home.

The morning after, Speedy got up early and climbed solo to the traverse, clearing the ropes, just enjoying the exercise. This was characteristic of him. He became bored lying around Base Camp and thrived on the action.

When he arrived back, Kiwi gave him a good talking-to, actually threatening to throw him off the expedition if he did anything like that again. Speedy hadn't taken a walkie-talkie with him. It seemed to me that Kiwi had things a little out of perspective. For Speedy to go up to the beginning of the traverse by himself was certainly not dangerous.

The weather on September 14 was clearing again. We discussed the possibility of going up the following day. It was a beautiful evening, cold and clear. But, as before, I was holding out for two days of clear

Bill March emerging from the icefall with the inevitable smile of relief. All of the climbers grew to both fear and respect the repeated trips through this awesome gateway to the mountain.

Additional ladders are carried up to replace those lost in crevasses and for use in bridging the crevasses in the Western Cwm.

Spearheaded by Al Burgess, in one day the Canadians, Sherpas, and New Zealanders push their way up to Camp I after a week of bad weather.

weather before we went back into the icefall, and this was only the first day. I resisted Kiwi's pressure to get on with it. I was very aware of the threatening avalanche conditions on the west shoulder.

We heard on the radio that evening that all the members who had left the expedition had now arrived in Kathmandu. John Amatt was priming them for their role as a cohesive group of returning heroes. This misrepresentation was resented in Base Camp. People had left for various reasons. I don't think John Amatt realized the repercussions of trying to present a picture that was not totally accurate. John also tried to make the case that we didn't need as many people because we were doing an easier route. In fact, it was the other way round. We were doing the easier route because we didn't have the manpower to do the more difficult one.

By September 15, a stable weather pattern was prevailing. The next day we would return to the mountain. It looked like Pat, Speedy, and I would be going. Laurie was leaving for Kunde to recuperate. Bill was already down valley. Kiwi planned to descend in a day or two. Dave Read would remain at Base Camp (bad back, low morale); Dwayne was still hesitating about his commitment. Peter Spear was still managing the day-to-day operation of Base Camp, and Steve Bezruchka and Bruce Patterson were helping him.

REOPENING THE ICEFALL

ON SEPTEMBER 16, we got up at 2:30 a.m. to cold, clear, and frozen conditions. Our loads were already up there, so Kiwi, Pat, Speedy, and I, plus the four New Zealanders, set out to the traverse. We covered the route very quickly.

When we got to the traverse, Kiwi took my rucksack. With four Sherpas, I went ahead to pull free and re-anchor the ropes in the traverse. In spite of some unstable ladders, we moved quickly. We found the last section of the traverse to be completely altered: big ice blocks leaning, crevasses opened, ladders fallen into the crevasses. Everything had to be re-fixed. This was done quickly, and we arrived at the beginning of what now was known as the "Valley of Death."

Continuing past the place where Pasang Sona's body had been found, we climbed over avalanche debris. Many of the ropes were impossible to pull free and we had to replace them. By now the Sherpas had dropped behind me and were replacing the rope while I pushed ahead without a load, breaking the trail up to the top of the debris. Here we uncovered about six loads previously left by the Sherpas who had been with Pat Morrow on the day of the avalanche.

We pressed on, pulling ropes until we got to the Prow, where our previously installed rope ladder went up onto a small plateau. It had taken four hours to reach this point—twice as long as previously, with broken trail and fixed ropes. At this point Kiwi turned back to Base Camp with all the Sherpas.

Three Canadians and four New Zealanders continued breaking trail into the upper section of the icefall. Some of the ropes were buried under four feet of new snow and laborious excavation was required. Eventually we arrived at a large, unbridged crevasse. The ladder had fallen down into it, and there remained one short piece frozen into the side. A 15-foot section was visible, 100 feet below on some blocks. Paul Moores used an icetool and rope to hook the ladder's rung, enabling us to fish it to the surface. This gave us a double ladder section that we could then refix.

This crevasse, however, was probably 30 feet wide and was impossible to bridge without a huge set of new ladders and handrail equipment, which we did not have. Down to the right there seemed to be a possibility—a narrower section with a rough ice and snow floor, jammed in about 20 feet below us. A large flake or fin of ice partially peeled from the opposite wall provided a sort of ramp that we could reach with our ladder. We fixed an anchor point and I rappelled into the bottom of the crevasse. I walked across it and Adrian threw the newly recovered ladder down to me. I leaned this up against the ice fin and, after it seemed secure enough, I scrambled up the ladder. Balancing on the top rung, I planted my ice tools. One big heave and I stood on easy ground on top of the fin. From there I reached the far edge of the crevasse and secured rope so that the others could follow. This provided a convenient variation for a few days. (Both the fin and the floor later disappeared into the abyss below.)

After everyone had come over this section, we retrieved the ladder for re-use. We would have to come back the next day to repair this section. We continued across two or three more bridges, still intact, and reached the newly opened crevasses of the final section—a very dangerous stretch of honeycombed ice. Adrian and I roped up and climbed in to explore. The groans and creaks were ominous. This and our observations quickly convinced us that the area was coming apart at an alarming rate. Crevasses were opening, bridges and ladders had fallen, and it looked as though the kind of collapse that had killed Blair Griffiths could happen again at any time. We decided to abandon the section and find a way around it.

Camp I is dug out and the climbers prepare to reopen and fix the route up to Camp II which had been reached by an advance party before the accidents.

A climber resting on his rucksack at Camp I after having carried a ladder through the icefall. In the background, one can look across the Lho La pass into Tibet.

By now the sun was very hot. We were all getting quite tired, wading around in the soft snow up to our knees. Adrian and I were breaking most of the trail. Again, it seemed the same old story. No one else was really prepared to come forward to help. Speedy was at the back, bringing forward ladders and packs (an essential role), so he could not be expected to replace a trail-breaker.

Adrian and I left our rucksacks and detoured around the edge of the crevassed section, up a slight rise and down again, in a big dog leg that brought us to the other side. This route seemed much easier and I couldn't think why we hadn't gone that way in the first place. Hindsight is twenty-twenty!

Camp I was now within reach. Only one more obstacle remained—a deep, steep-walled "valley" bottomed by a massive crevasse. On the other side we could see the pile of equipment under a snow-covered tarp. We had been in the icefall for 10 hours now. But our exploration had paid off—the dog leg was the key. We wound our way down to the crevasse, and Adrian started up the big slope on the far side. It was a huge crevasse, stretching the width of the Khumbu Icefall; it had been filled in at the bottom, and the steep sides were covered with new snow. Adrian slowly broke his way up this slope, unable to locate the old fixed rope. But, 200 feet higher, he found it and continued breaking up to Camp I. The sun was extremely hot, and most of us were suffering from sunburnt lips and noses and very dry throats.

The camp was a shambles, evidence that it had been left by climbers not expecting to return. Sleeping bags without stuff sacks had been thrown under tarpaulins, personal equipment was strewn around. An hour's digging was required before we could pull the tarpaulin off and get at the tents and cooking equipment. We flattened out an area and put up one of the Sportsman tents, anchoring it inside with big food boxes. We got a propane stove going to melt snow so that we could slake our extreme thirst. Everybody was exhausted, sitting motionless. Adrian and I put up a couple of tents before returning to make tea.

Peter Hillary said he felt really ill and I think he was suffering from extreme exertion, but after some food and some liquid he began to feel well again. After that day we seven hoped not to have to go back down.

We heard that evening that Bill March had just returned from Namche Bazaar. After our effort to reopen the icefall we hoped that all the people who were sitting in Base Camp waiting to see what would happen would now back us up more than verbally and get involved in trail-breaking and rope-fixing.

That evening was clear and cold, with a beautiful clear sunset over Pumori. It was comfortable to be in a tent with Adrian and Paul. I'd spent one expedition on Nanga Parbat with these two climbers and found their attitudes very similar to my own. They have a quiet drive and determination on the mountain. They know that they are world-class mountaineers and don't have anything to prove. They are easy-going and positive: they have a full appreciation of the dangers, but they don't exaggerate those dangers.

That evening we laughed and joked and realized that here we were together, supposedly part of two separate expeditions: one the Canadian "mega-trip" with all its trappings, the other in ethical opposition. Yet both had now been distilled to the verity of men and a mountain. It was a special moment. The mountain had sorted out who was here, who remained at Base Camp, and who had gone home.

Paul Moores, sitting with us tonight, had contracted a chest complaint at Base Camp and it was obvious that he was suffering. But he wasn't going to be left behind or wait for anyone else to do the work. He wanted to be where the action was.

SHERPA POWER

ON THE MORNING of September 17, we were up at 3:30 a.m., which took a lot of will power after the previous day's 10-hour struggle through the icefall. Adrian, Paul, and I headed out, breaking trail towards the "Nuptse corner," a massive avalanche outflow that touches the ends of large transverse crevasses and the Nuptse face. The crevasses force the route hard against the Nuptse wall, after a complex series of switchback traverses.

Here the Western Cwm is less than a thousand yards wide, and heavy snowfall is often followed by avalanches that sweep clean across it from either side. A central line would require a few more ladders and more effort, but it was still the safest way. Not safe, but safest.

Meanwhile, Speedy Smith, Fred From, Peter Hillary, and Pat Morrow went back down through the upper section of the icefall to fix the crevasses we had crossed the previous day and to hang a rope ladder into the ice fin crevasse. We had to do this before the Sherpas arrived. Twenty-one of them had left at 3:00 a.m., carrying loads and another ten were moving up to stay at Camp I. Bill accompanied them as far as the dog leg variation, fixing a drum of rope. Dwayne Congdon also came to Camp I to stay. By 8:00 a.m. Camp I became quite a busy place. In spite of its positive hustle and bustle, however, we were aware that there were still unresolved problems below.

Tea time at Camp I. Gordon Smith, Bill March, Al Burgess, and Dwayne Congdon ponder the problems ahead facing the expedition, now reduced to eight climbers.

The build-up of supplies continues at Camp I. Three additional trips were required to bring up needed Sherpa food, oxygen gear and communications equipment.

The west shoulder of Everest showing the lethal avalanche fracture.

Speedy wrote:

Dave is very demoralized about Caroline (no letters) so he is not coming up for a while. Kiwi has now gone down the valley for R&R. I don't think either Bill or Kiwi can stand the continuous strain of the responsibilities of leadership. Bill has more or less abdicated climbing leadership to Al. And I am looking after logistics. . . .

That afternoon, Speedy and I began sorting equipment and rounding up loads for the next day's carry to Camp II. The Sherpas, inventive as ever, dug a large pit in the snow, erected ladders as poles and a taut rope as a ridge, and covered the affair with a tarpaulin, forming a cool, spacious cooking shelter. They dug benches into the walls and covered them with pieces of plywood from the box tents. It was interesting to see that the Sherpas could also feel the altitude. We noticed them panting a little as they rushed around working.

The Western Cwm is a huge reflective oven. The afternoon heat at Camp I made sleep impossible, even lying in our underwear with sleeping bags thrown onto the tents—an odd situation considering we were camped on bottomless ice.

Now that the Sherpas were out of Base Camp they were elated. They had been told by the Sirdar, Gyaljen, that they would only be going as far as Camp III, after which they would be called back to be replaced by Sherpas waiting at Base Camp. But they realized that circumstances could change quickly enough, and they were happy to do their best.

The next morning, September 18, we were up at 2 a.m., beginning to feel the strain of the workload. Speedy, Dwayne, and Pat went to build a bridge over the large crevasse near the Nuptse corner to cut out 200 yards of dangerous terrain.

Nine Sherpas, the New Zealanders, and I made carries up to the site of Camp II at the head of the Western Cwm. I was roped up with Lhakpa Dorje, a small, chunky man who spoke very good English and who was acting Sirdar above Base Camp. We carried about 30 pounds each, as we moved up the glacier in the dark, along yesterday's zigzags to the Nuptse corner. After traversing left, back into the centre of the glacier, we made our way straight up towards Camp II. We found a safe site on the moraine at the edge of the glacier and thankfully dropped our loads.

Camp II was on the edge of a lateral moraine, among ridges of rock and gravel on top of hard ice, surrounded by crevasses. Covering this natural garbage pile is the human garbage of many past expeditions. The Sherpas scavenged around for booty. Namgyal found five ice screws. If they want to take the trouble to carry something they have found on the mountain down with them, then it's traditionally understood that they can keep it.

We made a quick run back down to Camp I and into the kitchen tent, out of the sun, for an 8 o'clock breakfast.

In the afternoon, Speedy and I were packing up loads again. A Sherpa who had been with us on Annapurna IV announced that he wanted to carry a load-and-a-half. This had an amazing effect on the rest of the Sherpas. Suddenly all wanted to do the same. The Sherpas threw item after item into their packs, shouting, "How much money now?" Then another item or two. "Now how much?" The joke grew to ridiculous but still somehow manageable proportions, adding as much to our spirit as to our progress.

After we had packed the loads, I lazed around with the Sherpas on the tarpaulin, backs against the loads, sitting on foam pads, chatting casually. They seemingly weren't affected by the heat or the sun and were sunbathing, drying out their double-bootliners, drinking tea, laughing, and joking. I found that after a little while they forgot I was there, and just accepted and ignored me, chatting away in Sherpa. If I wanted to know what they were saying, I would have to prod one of them and ask. I was getting very close to the Sherpas, finding it better to rope with them than with slower members of the expeditions. Further, the Sherpas didn't seem to play head games. In spite of the fun they had competing with each other, as exemplified by the extra half loads, they seemed somehow more graceful and open about it than we Westerners could be among ourselves.

The next day, September 19, we all got up a little later, at 3 a.m., and left at 4 a.m., carrying loads to Camp II. Dwayne, Pat, and Speedy roped together, and I climbed with the kitchen boy, Ang Lhakpa. Two of the strongest Sherpas, Pema Dorje and Sungdare, were going very quickly. They managed to carry 55 pounds each up to Camp II in only one hour and 40 minutes. With my 45 pounds, I took approximately two hours.

The route through the upper section of the Western Cwm is essentially unhindered by crevasses but the walls soar up to the sky on each side. The North Face of Nuptse was on our right, and the west shoulder of Everest was on our left. At the head of the Western Cwm, we saw the wind blowing over the summit ridge of Lhotse and the South Col. Descending from the South Col is the huge buttress of the Geneva Spur. Our route went just to the right of it. It was a majestic sight, "the highest valley in the world."

We dumped our loads. The weather was perfect, with bright blue cloudless sky, and it became very hot as we zigzagged back down round the crevasses to Camp I.

We heard over the radio that mail had arrived at Base Camp and that Bill was supposed to be coming up to Camp I to stay on the following day. In the afternoon, Speedy and I sorted out loads again for the morrow.

I was a little embarrassed by the fact that the Sherpas could carry so much weight day after day and still go faster than most of the climbers. I felt that they were actually taking us up the mountain. To gain back at least some respect, and maybe to make a point to some of the other Westerners, I decided to carry one of the large propane bottles. This is classed as a load-and-a-quarter at this altitude. It went into my rucksack to a sudden round of cheers and applause from the Sherpas. The image crossed my mind of a colonial bwana being applauded by natives for successfully picking a banana.

The next day, September 20, was a repeat of the previous day. Most of the Sherpas were taking very heavy loads. I roped up with Ang Lhakpa again, while Speedy roped up with Dwayne Congdon. Pat Morrow decided not to carry. I don't know why, but it had become one of the policies on this expedition that you did as you wanted, and no one questioned Pat's decision. The New Zealanders—Adrian, Peter, and Fred—moved up to Camp II to stay. Paul's chest infection persisted and he said that he would stay in Camp I to try to get rid of it.

When I arrived back at Camp I, I saw that Bill March had arrived to stay. He brought mail and was enthusiastic about the progress of the expedition.

Bill's diary recounts his feelings at this time:

It's almost as if each time, each step you make through the icefall, you have to summon that little extra effort from yourself, from within yourself, deep down, to go on.

It's really been an illuminating experience for me because I expect over the years . . . . the fear factor is decreased. It never disappears. . . . When you're afraid you're careful. But, for me, it was almost like starting all over again. I didn't sleep much that night before we went up the icefall. The second time through today I felt exactly the same and I know when I go up in a few days' time I'll feel the same way again.

It's almost as if one's psyche has been permanently scarred by it and it's quite a difficult experience. I think each man has had to find his own way of dealing with it.

I concentrated my energies on completing the final carries of food and equipment that would bring to an end the dangerous carries through the icefall. In all I made three carries with the

Sherpas. I was not willing to ask the members to travel through more than once. As leader I saw it clearly as my responsibility to demonstrate my commitment to the expedition.

September 21 was a rest day. Dwayne, Speedy, and I slept in. The Sherpas, however, chose to continue and carried more loads to Camp II. Bill and Pat went with them to shoot some video tape. We packed our personal gear and made up more Sherpa loads. Some were now carrying double loads, so the pile of gear was diminishing quickly. Speedy's and my plan had allocated 15 days to move everything to Camp II, but it now looked as though it would take half that time. The Sherpa rate was almost fulfilling a secret plan I knew they had to complete the climb in 10 days. The rest day gave us a chance for discussions. Bill obviously wanted to get a fresh grip on the leadership.

Wednesday, September 22, we were up at 3:30 a.m. Speedy wrote:

The way is ingrained in my memory now, a few sweeping zigzags to the ladder poking out of the snow, then the rollercoaster up and down to the triple ladder at the Nuptse corner. A few more zigzags and then break out into the Western Cwm proper, a long trail straight up left until eventually just as you are dropping with exhaustion, veer off to the left onto the moraine. Get your breath back here and a last plod up a long groove between the glacier and the moraine to Camp II on top of the rocks.

I was well out in front with Ang Lhakpa. When we arrived at Camp II we sat down and rested, waiting for the others. The Sherpas all came in with their personal gear and we started to set up camp. It was difficult to visualize this rubble heap as the colourful tent village it was soon to become. But it happened, and after a couple of days every crevasse and large rock became familiar. We were no longer fighting the mountain but had become part of it.

This was Advance Base Camp, a substantial establishment. It was the high point for the 16' x 8' x 6' metal-framed insulated Weatherport hut. We set our tents around it as the focal point of the site. The six-by-six Sportsman tent became the kitchen, except in extreme wind, when it had to be dismantled. We put food boxes around the inside of the Weatherport as seats and in one corner a propane bottle and double-burner stove. It was not as stifling here as in Camp I, and we could wander around in down jackets with just our underwear on. The New Zealand expedition was already established at Camp II. They had taken over the North Star tent and a couple of Woods dome tents. The establishment of Camp II was complete. The Lhotse face loomed above.

Ravens wait outside a tent at Camp I (19,500'). Across a foreground of gaping crevasses the summit of Pumori emerges from a sea of cloud. Pumori (23,442') was climbed in 1978 by two members of the Canadian team—Lloyd Gallagher and Tim Auger.

Looking up the Western Cwm at climbers and Sherpas descending from Camp II. The line of crevasses behind the climbers faces the route to below the Nuptse face.

We now had expedition members spread all the way from here to somewhere near Kunde, two-and-a-half days below Base Camp. Camp II had Speedy, Pat, me, the four New Zealanders, and four Sherpas. At Camp I were Bill, Dwayne, Dave Read and Kiwi and a number of Sherpas. Steve Bezruchka, Kurt Fuhrich and Peter Spear were at Base Camp and Laurie Skreslet was somewhere down the valley.

The New Zealanders were the spearhead, pushing 450 feet of new rope up the steep Lhotse face on September 22.

THE YAK ROUTE

THE AGREEMENT with the New Zealanders was a meagre attempt to straighten out in the field a very complex ethical and practical problem. Its full implications are still under heated discussion in some circles. The details of this pact, however, had already begun to disturb me as early as September 22, when we established Camp II in fine weather and were faced with the prospect of an eight-day wait before moving further. Since the Canadian and New Zealand tents at this stage formed one small communal village, I stepped next door to further complicate the complications.

This visit started two days of renegotiation in worsening weather, with the September 30 deadline drawing closer, and compromises had to be made on both sides. Finally, agreement was reached to climb together. The mountain had contributed once more to our decision.

On September 23, the New Zealand team left at approximately 7:30 a.m. It was much colder up here and there wasn't the same necessity to leave before daybreak. The rest of our Sherpas from Camp I arrived with Bill March and Dwayne Congdon to stay at Camp II. Kiwi Gallagher and Dave Read arrived on an acclimatization walk, carrying light loads, intending to return to Camp I the same evening and possibly come back up within the next few days.

We could hear the wind roaring over the west shoulder of Everest and I realized that the post-monsoon weather had arrived. The wind would gradually worsen until the winter season began. But I also knew that, as the wind changes direction, there are often periods of a few days with very little wind. You have to be in the right place at the right time to take advantage of these breaks.

Peter and Fred from the New Zealand team managed to fix another 450 feet of rope. They came back to camp with tales of extremely strong winds and blowing snow, producing waves of spindrift. We heard on the radio that the Catalan expedition on the West Ridge of

Everest was trying to reach their Camp III but had been driven back by the wind.

On that day, my brother and I shared a birthday, celebrated with Canadians and New Zealanders alike in the comfort of the Weatherport hut. It seemed strange having a birthday up there, especially with a twin brother with whom I had spent the day locked in heavy negotiations. Bill opened a bottle of Canadian Club and the Catalans sang "Happy Birthday" over the radio.

September 24 was very windy. No progress was advisable above Camp II. It was becoming apparent that a steady stream of lower and lower priority material was trickling through the icefall, with increasingly casual requests for supplementary items. It was time to draw a line. We therefore determined that the loads in Camp II were sufficient and closed the icefall to further passage. Laurie Skreslet created an exception for himself by coming through solo, but the main intent was to keep Sherpas out of the danger zone.

We realized later that our action was seen by the world below as a heroic severance from possible retreat. This was amusing in retrospect. Although the closure had some of that implication, the greater reality was that it freed our concentration for the route above.

Bill wrote:

It's a funny feeling being up here—kind of cut off from the outside world. Our only contact is the radio to Base Camp. Because we have a limited supply of batteries, we're restricting that to one call a day at 6:00. It's just weird being up here, being cut off in this way. You feel committed and you look ahead and see what's ahead of you —boy, it's a lot of climbing, a lot of effort and a lot of early morning starts and cold discomfort and the sheer drudgery of making the body do things, just screaming in protest, it doesn't want to do.

The challenge now was to push rope to 26,000 feet at the South Col. I could sense that many of the people in the expedition were beginning to tire, although we'd only been up here 10 days or so and were likely to be here another 10 days. This expedition, I considered, was a cruise compared to Dhaulagiri or Annapurna IV, where we were working 10 days straight without a rest.

Bill wrote:

You certainly need something up there. It's extremely physically demanding to be working in such thin air. You walk 10 paces and

Solar cell panels were used to charge the batteries of the video cameras at Camp II.

Camp II on the lateral moraine at the top of the Western Cwm. This is the traditional site of Camp II and the debris of previous expeditions was much in evidence.

then you rest, you walk 10 paces, then you rest. Any hard work like carrying a load or breaking trail is really a fantastic effort. . . . You really do begin to feel the altitude. The best way to describe it is to add 20 years onto your life. You walk around like an old man, especially if you've got a load on your back.

Dave Read and Kiwi Gallagher, still at Camp I, were also feeling drained, although they didn't voice it. Kiwi was beginning to look very drawn.

Speedy Smith, by contrast, was in a lyrical mood on the evening of the 25th:

It feels warm outside and I can see a half-moon above Nuptse which is in shadow. The silvery moon glow is cast over the West Face of Lhotse and the South West Face of Everest. The stars are out and rock crags seem to stand out from the snow slopes like medieval castles. Everything is so still, just the sigh of the wind high up against the ridges of Everest to remind you that this is not a painting nor a dream.

Speedy was able to continue working day after day and still keep something in reserve. Maybe it's because he was a little older than most of the people on the expedition that he was able to recover quickly. He was also carrying a little extra weight, which seemed to give him extra staying power. I felt, looking at him, that he could have gone on for another two or three weeks without any problem, whereas some of the others obviously needed a rest.

Bill's notes recorded the general feeling at this stage of the expedition:

What we'd all like to do is just climb this mountain and get home to our wives and families. We have been away a long time now, over two months and the mountain is still there. . . . It's a big under-taking, but we'll push on. . . . It's not like an alpine climb where one exerts oneself for maybe two or three days at the most, pushing and facing a lot of danger. Up here on Everest we face it every day, every single day, day in and day out, week in and week out.

Maybe some of the less experienced members were demoralized because they felt we were making a show of carrying on with the expedition, while not really expecting to climb the mountain. In fact it was still September and we had lots of time left.

Bill considered it much easier to lead now that the team was so much smaller. He wrote, "It was as though the mountain had brought about what was necessary. Instead of an unwieldy, diverse group there was suddenly a compact, cohesive unit and that was what was needed." I think that, earlier in the expedition, many of the less experienced people wanted their opinions to be taken into account. Now, high up in the Western Cwm, most of the expedition members were beyond their level of expertise and were prepared to follow the leadership of more experienced climbers.

Bill's new optimism was apparent in his diary:

You realize you're quite a privileged person, a really privileged person to be here with these men engaged in this undertaking. It's something that only happens maybe once or twice in a lifetime. Whatever is going on down there in the world and whatever people think and feel . . . up here is reality. Up here is comradeship, sharing, danger, careful judgment, hard work, and perhaps the answer to what life is all about. Perhaps . . ."

The first Canadian moves on the Lhotse face were made when Adrian and I fixed ropes up to and past the Camp III site. It was great to be active again. We followed the easy glacier up for about an hour to the Bergschrund (the large crevasse at the juncture of the glacier and the face), following a well-wanded trail. Climbing over the Bergschrund we took turns in the lead to the top of the fixed rope.

Then Adrian pushed rope 800 feet higher. Sungdare, Pema and I joined him at the new anchor, near a small ice bulge to the right of the route. This would provide some protection from powder avalanches, and seemed a good site for Camp III. Sungdare and Pema descended. I led out another 450-foot drum leftwards into the centre of the couloir, aiming in the most direct line for the yellow rock band that traverses the Lhotse face.

Dave Read, Kiwi, and Laurie moved up from Camp I to join the expedition. Laurie brought up some mail which informed us that Roger Marshall had been interviewed in Canada and that we now had many critics in the media. But at least there were some telegrams: from Lord Hunt, leader of the first ascent in 1953, and from a number of other people wishing us luck.

There was still a strong feeling against the people who had left the expedition. What seemed ironic to me was that the loudest criticism was coming from the more recent arrivals. I knew that some of the men who had left did far more work than some who had stayed. It was one

The view down the
Western Cwm from
Camp II. The lower
valley was often in cloud
while the sun shone higher
on the mountain.

The view from Camp II
up the Western Cwm
looking onto the south face
of Lhotse. Everest dome
tents are secured in the
foreground.

thing to have decided to stay on the expedition and apparently quite another to make an active effort toward getting somebody to the top. Furthermore, it was only as a lightened expedition that we could progress as well as we had.

September 27 was not very productive. A mistake in communications in high winds resulted in about 400 feet of rope above the Camp III site being placed too far to the right. Nevertheless, Speedy and some Sherpas dug a ledge and secured a number of loads. He, Fred From, and Dwayne Congdon descended, very cold and tired. They were followed by an equally tired Laurie Skreslet, and still later by New Zealanders Peter Hillary and Paul Moores, also exhausted. We had all expended a lot of energy with discouragingly little result.

We heard on the radio that night that one of the Sherpas on the Catalan West Ridge expedition had died of suspected peritonitis. One of our Sherpas now became head of the dead man's family, and wished to return home to sort out funeral arrangements. We arranged for him to go down the next day with Paul Moores, who had still not recovered from his chest infection and needed a rest.

On September 28th when Adrian and I fixed rope above Camp III, it appeared the South Col objective would take longer than we first anticipated. We had to push harder. Aid, Lhapka Tshering, Lhapka Dorje and I moved quickly up to the foot of the fixed ropes and, without stopping to rest, continued directly to Camp III and on to the previous day's anchor, 200 feet above. From there I led until I ran out of anchors. Adrian ascended to the top of yesterday's misplaced rope, retrieved some, and rejoined me within 30 minutes. That was superb speed at this altitude and under these wind-harassed conditions.

While I was waiting for him, I contemplated the position I was in. I was looking up diagonally leftwards to the Geneva Spur and the Yellow Band. Wave after wave of powder spindrift surged by me. We had to be very careful fixing rope in this kind of weather. One mistake of balance and we would be hurtling down the face. The anchors were good when pulled from below, but not strong enough to resist the shock of a fall.

Adrian brought the anchors and I led out, slowly working my way diagonally across the couloir, always heading for the weakness in the Yellow Band, intermittently visible through ice-crusted goggles and surging swells of driving snow.

Adrian joined me at the belay, then took over the lead. I was proud of my brother's rhythmic, effortless progress with a minimum amount of protection in these conditions and I took several photographs of him at work.

Looking down across the couloir, I could see a lone figure moving very slowly across the fixed rope into the centre of the couloir. On closer observation I could see that it was Kiwi Gallagher. I looked back up, the ropes quickly running through my hands, at Adrian disappearing up the slope. This, for me, is what expeditions are all about: the climbing, the rhythm, the deep breathing, the blood pounding through lungs and veins, and the feeling of moving powerfully over steep ground with the new horizon unfolding before you and the Bergschrund dropping away, way down towards the lower camps. When I arrived to join Adrian, I cut a step in the snow and stood there, hardly needing to communicate with him, we had done this so many times before. Adrian led out more rope. Kick, kick, a stab with the axe, a side step here, a balance upwards, sideways on the crampon points, completely relaxed, letting the rhythm of the climb absorb the mind.

That day we fixed 1,400 feet of rope. Adrian came sliding back down to me. "Well youth, let's get down. We're out of anchors. Not a bad day's work."

Pat and Bill had moved up to occupy Camp III, in preparation for fixing more rope the following day. The filming of the expedition didn't seem to be going too well and that evening we got a concerned radio call from John Amatt in Kathmandu. He would like someone to try to shoot video tape high on the mountain. Nobody dared to tell him that the video camera was buried under three feet of snow at Camp III. People were having enough trouble looking after themselves without shooting tapes.

On September 29, Bill March and Pat Morrow set out to push up rope. Pat was going much slower, having trouble with his oxygen. He turned back. An avalanche had torn away 400 feet of rope on the traverse towards the Yellow Band. Bill refixed it, then led up through the Yellow Band, on oxygen. He wrote later, "It was minus 40 degrees— hard ice and brittle—and I placed a screw after 150 feet to protect my ascent. I traversed right on thin ice, failed to place a second screw and eventually pushed on upwards to some snow."

Two Sherpas came more slowly, carrying loads up the rope behind him. Bill was now really beginning to put out. He realized there weren't many people working effectively high on the mountain and that if he wanted to be productive he would have to use oxygen. He pressed on and ran out over 1000 feet of rope that day, quite high above the rock band. ". . . a wave of emotion swept through me . . . almost as if my destiny had been fulfilled. I knew in my heart this would be my high point—my climbing contribution to the expedition had almost ended . . . and it was up to Alan and the others to take it on."

Life at Camp III was certainly not comfortable. As Speedy Smith described it:

> It's very cold when we awaken at 5:30 and very windy. Menus we have here aren't very appetizing, but we do manage to eat tea and granola. Where the hell are those kippers that Peter Spear promised us? He said they were already on the hill. I think somebody else must have eaten them. We dig ourselves out of the tent and I find it very difficult to move outside in this wind and spindrift. The Sun Ice suits are not really suitable for answering the calls of nature. The zips are hidden under too much velcro and can't be pulled apart with numb hands. In the end I have to return to the box tent and take the suit off.

Speedy was also having trouble getting his oxygen equipment to function after the two men who had been up with oxygen the day before left the equipment in the snow. He spent hours trying to defrost it while Pema and Sungdare proceeded without oxygen.

The oxygen equipment Dwayne Congdon was to use was also frozen. Impatient to get going, he left it behind and tried to carry on without oxygen.

As Speedy continued to struggle with his oxygen equipment, Kiwi Gallagher arrived from Camp II and carried on towards the Yellow Band. Eventually, Speedy managed to get his mask sorted out and set off after Kiwi. The effect of bottled oxygen was remarkable. Speedy reported:

> While it's working, it's fantastic. Kiwi is halfway across the traverse when I leave Camp III and I overtake him before the end. Then I pick up a spool of bluewater rope, anchors, screws and carabiners . . . so I have a heavy load. I still gain on Dwayne even though the oxygen alternatively sticks on full and sometimes doesn't work at all.

Both Dwayne and Speedy continued until Pema and Sungdare came down. They had fixed rope to within 200 feet of the South Col. This was an absolutely fantastic effort by two of the strongest Sherpas I've ever worked with. Sungdare knows how to fix snow anchors and ice screws faster and better than most Westerners. Speedy and Dwayne had reached about 25,000 feet.

After Bill had used oxygen he felt confident that even he might be able to reach the summit. We began to see the first symptoms of what is commonly known as Everest Fever. A plan was developing to try to reach the summit within the next two days. The plan would involve

The Lhotse face showing team members climbing towards Camp III. To the left of the stepped-in cliffs the long avalanche chute can be discerned. An avalanche sweeping down wiped out several hundred feet of fixed line.

contiguous roping and carrying parties, followed by Bill and Kiwi as summiteers. I found it interesting that the desire to reach the summit of the world's highest mountain could often drive people to take risks that they would not normally take and lose perspective about the expedition as a whole.

Speedy wrote: "Bill and Kiwi are gung ho about oxygen and think, provided the Sherpas can carry enough oxygen, they can do it. In reality they are putting the clock back ethically 30 years." At this point, the matter of climbing ethics didn't really seem to enter into it. It was becoming a political climb with political objectives. We had to reach the summit at all costs, no matter how.

That evening, in the Weatherport tent, we all sat around and discussed plans. I could feel that most people now wanted to get up the mountain and get off. They wanted me to make a summit bid as soon as possible.

This attitude angered me. They were talking about a critical combination of altitude, oxygen, and energy with which they had little experience. You don't rush to the summit of Everest without proper acclimatization. The snows of the upper slopes hide many bony remains of such naive hubris. The time would come when I would be ready, and so would others on this expedition. But we weren't there yet. Still, when I hesitated, others saw it as timidity, and eagerly jumped in to climb what they saw as the fixed path to success. As Adrian said, "Suddenly every man and his dog wanted to go to the summit."

Bill and I were sharing a tent at this time, so I was able to observe the confidence he exuded in the group setting, but was also able to share his personal doubts about a rash summit bid.

This inconsistency is very understandable and certainly not unique to Bill. In mountaineering you often see people tantalized by the chance to step outside the limits of their own normal self-image. It is heady stuff, and small considerations like safety, group ethics, and loyalties can pale by comparison. It's a time to be wary. Two vital things are at stake: human life, which can be lost to carelessness, and human dignity, which can be lost in the scramble to achieve success by sacrificing ideals.

Fortunately, on October 1 the winds were very high and the two-day plan was abandoned. I think Bill was quite relieved.

That day, seven Sherpas carried loads to Camp III and my brother Adrian and Laurie Skreslet moved up to Camp III to stay. We had almost enough equipment there now. We were just waiting to get the rope to the South Col so that we could have a rest and make the final push to the summit.

JUST ONE ROPE MORE

ON OCTOBER 1, Adrian got to 25,800 feet in only three-and-a-half hours. Laurie Skreslet, even though he wasn't carrying a rucksack, couldn't even make it to the end of the ropes and by the time Adrian was descending the ropes Laurie gave up, at about 24,500 feet. That evening a very chastened Laurie returned to Advance Base Camp. The reality of the situation was gradually being brought home to the climbers, and they all began to realize how much they were going to need to rely upon supplementary oxygen.

That evening Paul Moores and their Sirdar from Base Camp, Phu Tenzing, arrived with mail. This was the last time anyone came up from Base Camp.

At high anchor, 200 feet from the South Col, we and the New Zealanders parted ways. They went right towards Lhotse; we went left to the South Col. So far, our group's high-altitude performance, with or without oxygen, had not been very reassuring. The severe wind and spindrift were constant obstacles. Laurie Skreslet had been forced back without oxygen and both Speedy Smith and Pat Morrow had had problems with oxygen equipment. It was starting to look as if we might have trouble getting rope out to the South Col.

I woke up at 4:00 a.m. on the morning of October 3, and the wind was still wildly tearing at the camp. I climbed out of the tent and went to speak to the Sherpas. I had been planning to go with Sungdare and Lhakpa Dorje, but after they heard the wind around the tents they were very reluctant to get out of their sleeping bags. They thought that if we went out on a day like this it would be a wasted effort. I told them that we didn't need to leave early; I would wake them up again at 7:00 a.m. and we could try to leave shortly afterwards. Maybe by that time the wind would have dropped. Even though we might not reach the South Col, it would be a good opportunity to acclimatize.

If the weather continued like this, the general feeling was that we would end up going back down to Base Camp for a rest before making the final summit attempt. In fact, when I left that morning, my understanding was that if the bad weather did continue, we would probably all go down for four days' rest. Following that, I would be making the first summit attempt with Lhakpa Dorje and Sungdare.

At 7:00 a.m. the weather hadn't really improved much, but at least now it was daylight and looking a little friendlier outside. The Sherpas hadn't moved from their sleeping bags, and it seemed obvious that they did not consider the day good enough to fix rope. However, I managed

Sherpas and climbers struggle with wind and spindrift to cut out a platform and pitch the box tent at Camp III (23,500'). This tent later had to be dug out and reset by Laurie Skreslet and others.

Camp III safely established on the south face of Lhotse with the southwest face of Everest in the background. The tents were protected by a small ice cliff above from the threat of avalanche.

Bill March brewing up in Camp III. Altitude climbing requires a high fluid intake to maintain adequate hydration, one of the most effective defences against altitude illness.

The view down the Western Cwm from Camp III at dusk. Such moments of beauty are part of the rewards of high altitude climbing.

to coax them to get up and have a drink of tea and some tsampa porridge. I said that we could always go part way and see what developed.

We stomped quickly across the glacier towards the Bergschrund and within two hours were again at Camp III. Without stopping, we continued up the fixed ropes. I was travelling about 100 feet behind the Sherpas so that all three of us wouldn't be suspended from the same snow anchor. When Sherpas go up fixed ropes, they have a habit of moving directly behind one another, confident that no matter how many people hang on, it will hold.

We pushed slowly upward and I was gradually losing ground to the Sherpas. By the time I got above the Yellow Band they were almost 200 feet ahead. They collected more coils of rope on the way, and were still going strong, even with the extra weight, to the end of the fixed ropes at 25,800 feet.

By now I was approximately 400 feet behind. Without having to be told, Sungdare unravelled more rope and began to lead the last 200 feet to the South Col. By the time I reached Lhapka Dorje, Sungdare was already anchored 150 feet from the South Col. One more rope length and we'd be there! I stood around with Lhapka Dorje, waiting, until I realized that these two Sherpas were in complete control of the situation. It was like climbing with some of the best and strongest of my climbing friends. They understood what had to be done and how to do it without unnecessary risk.

I felt the blood pounding in my head. I was not using oxygen. A slight aching persisted in the back of my skull. The Sherpas would soon have the 150 feet of rope fixed to the South Col without my help or direction. Lhakpa Dorje and I quickly agreed on the route. "Yes, Al. We come to the edge, fix the rope, and we'll be back down straight away."

With that, I turned and began to move back down. I stopped a couple of hundred feet lower and looked back. Sungdare had almost reached the South Col now, and within 15 minutes he would be chasing me back down the ropes. I stepped quickly and carefully down the slope, with the rope wrapped around my upper arm and clipped to my harness. I could see all the way down to Camp I and almost to Base Camp. I had taken five-and-a-half hours without oxygen to come from Camp II to 25,800 feet. I felt that was good for acclimatization and would help me move even more strongly the next time I was up.

On and on down the ropes. Descending through the Yellow Band, I was particularly careful. An ice screw into thin water ice was all that supported the rope. On and on, down and down. Back across the traverse to Camp III and then running more and more quickly down towards the Western Cwm. When I arrived at the Bergschrund, I could

OVERLEAF

Lhakpa Tshering and Bill March fixing ropes above Camp III. The rope was parceled out in 400' lengths by a climber who in turn anchored it with snow stakes.

High altitude Sherpa Lhakpa Tshering coming up the fixed rope through the Yellow Band above Camp III. Behind one can look down the immense expanse of the Western Cwm.

Al Burgess crossing the Geneva Spur with the face of Nuptse in the background.

see Lhakpa Dorje and Sungdare already well into their descent. I decided to wander back across to Camp II without waiting for them, knowing that these two Sherpas would not take risks and were much safer than most teams on this mountain.

I felt very tired as I entered Camp II. Speedy Smith said it was the first time he had seen me this tired, and I realized that I needed a day or so of rest. Base Camp would certainly be the best place for that. I had been above Base Camp now for 18 days. I was tired at that moment, but I still felt that as time wore on I was getting more and more acclimatized. Provided that I could keep eating to keep my strength up, I felt I could sustain this effort for at least two more weeks. After all, compared to winter expeditions, this was a cruise. We had reasonable food and lots and lots of liquid. Most of the heavy carrying was being done by the Sherpas.

I soon discovered that there had been changes in the wind, both literally and figuratively. The constant howl and spindrift were now certainly decreasing, providing the opportunity for an immediate summit bid. Bill had been agonizing over which Canadians and Sherpas, and in what combination, would be sent, and I felt he must be thankful that the weather and logistics had almost made a decision for him. Laurie Skreslet, Lhakpa Dorje and Sungdare were the obvious choices in Camp II at this moment. I would have liked a shot, too, of course, but I knew I was in no shape for an attempt the very next morning. Dave Read and Kiwi Gallagher were also keen to see how high they could get. I was concerned about the possible results of this, but I was too tired to worry very much about other people's problems and went to bed.

IT'S GONNA BE US THREE

LAURIE SKRESLET stayed up, preparing his equipment for what he regarded not specifically as a summit attempt, but rather, as a push to establish Camp IV. That evening, he half-hoped to catch sight of a strange visitor he had first seen a couple of nights earlier. As he described the incident:

All the Canadians were in bed, and a full moon was out. I like to wait up now and then in the evenings to see the full moon, it was beautiful, and all the Sherpas were up in the tent, up above, singing and dancing. . . . I was there for half an hour, and then I noticed, way down in the valley, the Western Cwm, clouds coming up, just starting to move up the valley, but low, you know, maybe 200 feet above the glacier, and I watched them snake up the glacier, it took

159

about seven to eight minutes. . . . Nice and slow and everything, until maybe halfway to the top of Nuptse. And then [they] just took the form of an angel, of a figure with a robe on, with the arms spread out. I'm not that religious, but it looked like an angel, arms spread, looking down on Camp II. I wasn't scared but I wanted to tell somebody, you know, but everyone was asleep, and the Sherpas were up in the tent, singing and dancing. By the time I got up there to bring someone out, it'd be too late. It was there for 10 . . . or 15 seconds . . . and then it disappeared into thin air, the clouds just dissipated, while the lower clouds stayed.

I thought, well, maybe it's a good sign. Maybe it means we're being watched. I put it out of my mind. But I slept good that night. I felt really calm inside. I didn't feel any fear.

Laurie and all the Sherpas left at 4:00 a.m. on October 4. They reached Camp III at daybreak. Laurie retrieved a bottle and an oxygen apparatus there.

It was blowing again and I had to get a shovel to cut out an entrance to one of the tents, and dug around, and pulled out an oxygen bottle. I had never used an oxygen set before. I don't think I had even put a mask on my face. I kept thinking, hum! I sure hope this sucker works!

When the Sherpas started moving on up, Laurie decided that the last thing he wanted was to be the last on that line:

I wanted to be with those guys when we got to the col. So I grabbed the bottle, pulled out all that apparatus, stuck it in my pack. I wanted to be in the middle, so that if I had trouble with the system or I was moving slow . . . with Sherpas behind me, I thought they'd be constantly an inspiration to keep moving. Their speed was something I could regulate mine at.

His first experience with oxygen was not encouraging. As he said later:

So I set off, got the mask working, but the bloody mask didn't fit my face. The only way to get the mask to work properly was to squeeze it so bloody tight that it pinched my nose; it felt like my nose was cut right across the top. I had to keep pushing the mask tight to my face. There was a gap, air kept coming out, and it was such a hassle. . . . I stopped three times trying to get it figured out. Finally I got it working to what *I* thought was satisfactory. And I just didn't take it off again after that.

He tucked in with some Sherpas, and stayed with them, experimenting with the oxygen set. He used the loaded Sherpas, who were not using oxygen, as a measure. But when he stopped to give some headache tablets to two Sherpas who were in pain, he noticed that Paul Moores, on the New Zealand team, was coming up several hundred feet behind. Laurie noticed that Paul did not have oxygen. Yet, no matter how Laurie pushed, it seemed he couldn't move further away from Paul.

Paul Moores beneath me, that was the sort of thing that was keeping *me* going. And I wanted to go to 26,000 feet *without* oxygen, to prove to myself that I had some kind of safety margin. If there was an emergency I might be able to do *something* for myself. But to go right from Camp III on oxygen left a big question mark there. That question mark was bugging me when I saw Paul Moores coming up behind me, and I was still having trouble. It caused me to worry. . . . If a guy without oxygen can be moving as fast as me *with* it, I wondered, you know, what am I doing? Am I walking to my death?

Laurie eventually did move away from Paul, however, feeling better. He passed some Sherpas at the Yellow Band, and by the upper sections, was moving quickly. He, Sungdare, and Lhakpa Dorje were among the first, at 12:30, to the South Col. The other Sherpas arrived within the next 15 or 20 minutes. Camp IV was assembled quickly and everyone left again, leaving Laurie, Sungdare, and Lhakpa Dorje alone up there.

Laurie wandered around, picking up oxygen bottles, trying to find out which ones had any air in them. His aim was to find sleeping oxygen, so that their full bottles could be saved for climbing. The empty bottles he tied onto his tent cords as additional weight. Once the tent was secure, he got into it, knocked all the snow off his boots, cleaned off his clothes, snapped the frost liner in, zipped the tent up, and fired up a hanging stove. "I made sure the copper band was on because this was *my* pride and joy and none of these guys was using it. I made sure it was on this one!" (The hanging apparatus and copper fuel heater were Laurie's design, and the fuel heater's "indispensability" had not gained universal team acceptance.)

He blew up four Thermorests and arranged them against the walls for insulation. When the Sherpas were finished, they came into his tent. It was about 2:30 p.m. The Sherpas ate, but Laurie didn't have an appetite.

We just sat there and drank and drank and drank [tea] and talked about the morning and where we were going to go and the time we

*The view of Everest from
above Camp III at
24,000'.*

*Ascending the fixed ropes
on the Lhotse face.*

*Sherpas on the Lhotse
face. The high altitude
Sherpas worked hard to
ensure the success of the
expedition.*

should leave, and then I'd look out, and I'd look at my watch. And finally I said, "Well, it looks to me like it's gonna be us three."

It was now 5:30 p.m. The others obviously had turned back. Sungdare said he planned to do the summit and get back to Camp II in one day. He said the weather looked good.

About 5:45, Laurie said good night to the Sherpas. He decided not to have dinner, just to go to sleep. He calculated: "I'm gonna get from six to twelve, it'll be six hours, and get up at two o'clock, that's eight . . . I'll have *eight hours of sleep*. I thought, Wow! Will that be good! I thought, *All right! It's in the bag! I'm gonna do this baby! Gonna do it!*"

The only remaining chore was the agreed-upon 6:00 p.m. radio check with Camp II. Laurie called.

Camp II wanted to know if Dave Read and Kiwi Gallagher had arrived at Camp IV.

"Negative."

It looked like they had an emergency. The two men were missing between Camps III and IV. When someone in Camp II asked, "How high is Kiwi going?" Adrian replied wryly, "He might be going a lot higher than he thinks."

Laurie said later:

I thought, Oh wow! Give me a break! You're kidding! Everything was set. . . . The chances looked *so* good. I didn't want to really admit to myself we were gonna do it but . . . how could you ask for anything better ? . . . The weather, the best Sherpas you could ever ask for, been to the summit twice before, the weather's good, you've got full oxygen bottles . . . and he's saying you gotta go out and look for them, and I thought. Oh no! There goes the summit.

Laurie realized that the search would use three full oxygen bottles. Once they started out there was no telling how long they would be gone, or how much Kiwi or Dave would need if they found them.

Laurie alerted the two Sherpas, who started putting on their gear with an air of resignation. Laurie helped them with their oxygen sets and headlamps, until all three were set to go. And then:

Just when we were all set to take off . . . who should come stumbling into camp . . . covered in hoar frost but Dave, and I thought, Oh no! I don't *believe* this . . . why'd he keep pushing up to here? . . . I said, "Hey, gee, good to see ya" and I'm thinking, What the hell are ya doing, you . . .

*Oxygen bottles, the debris
of previous expeditions,
litter the South Col.
Above, the final 3000 feet
of Everest present the final
challenge to the expedition.*

*Al Burgess traversing from
the Geneva Spur to the
South Col.*

Camp IV on the South
Col which was reached by
five members of the
Canadian team. From here
the two summit bids were
mounted.

Early morning light at
Camp IV.

Laurie pulled Dave's pack off, got him into the tent, put an oxygen mask on him, and pulled his crampons off. He was thinking, what if Dave hadn't reached here? He would have *died*! Why didn't he go down back at three or four o'clock? He set up a radio set for Sungdare and Lhakpa Dorje to use, and kept working with Dave. He got some food and drink heating, and then raised Bill March on the radio. Laurie told Bill that he would stay with Dave, and that the two Sherpas could be co-ordinated by radio from Camp II. Dave was very tired, talking slowly, and definitely needed help. Bill agreed.

From Camp II, Bill and I took over direction of the Sherpas. We told them that there were two oxygen bottles at the Lhotse Camp IV site, and they'd have to get there, to the last point that Dave had seen Kiwi. We knew that if he wasn't there he had to be on his way down. But it was pitch black. He had been out *14 hours*. That meant his oxygen wasn't working, or had quit by now, because Dave Read had already run out. He was without oxygen, and we knew he wasn't up to it.

We told the Sherpas to sweep the ropes back to Camp III. What has happened on other expeditions is that people get to a point where they are so tired that they have to go on a figure of eight (rappel device), so they take a glove off to attach it, and they drop the glove because they're not quite alert. Then their fingers start to freeze, and they can't take the figure of eight off to change it around, so they end up freezing on the rope. Even if Kiwi were unconscious, he could be saved if the Sherpas found him quickly, got him on oxygen, and kept him warm. He might lose fingers, but they could at least get him down alive.

The Sherpas hadn't descended far, however, before Kiwi came onto the radio, and we could just make out his light. We ordered Sungdare and Lhakpa Dorje back up to Camp IV. They could still make a summit bid.

Kiwi assured us that he could get down to Camp III by himself. We were not entirely convinced and continued to worry, monitoring the speck of his headlamp until we were sure he'd arrived at Camp III.

Kiwi's diary account reveals a rather different perspective:

By now it was getting on in the evening.

Dave was just in front of me and I wasn't sure if he was going to go on to Camp IV and return, but it looked like he could make Camp IV that night as well. I recalled his desire to make his ultimate goal the South Col. . . . Only a limited amount of oxygen was available, it was getting dark and there were only four sleeping bags at Camp IV. These would now be used by Laurie, Dave, and the two Sherpas.

170

The view along the ridge
from the south summit to
the main summit — one
hour from the top.

Climbers slowly moving
up the summit ridge.
Makalu is in background
and Kanchenjunga on the
horizon.

I started the return trip to Camp III. I was very disappointed as I still felt very strong and had come so close, but I certainly didn't want to jeopardize my life any more, even though conditions were perfect and there was very little wind. I did not feel overwhelmed by conditions or elevation. There was no question in my mind that had I been forced to spend a night out at this elevation, I would have no problems surviving.

Just as I started to descend the ropes to Camp III, I heard from the Base Camp radio and Camp II that they were worried about my whereabouts as darkness was closing in. I was out of reach by radio contact and couldn't advise anyone of my presence. Radio contact could not be made until I came within sight of Camp II, which was about 700 feet down the fixed ropes. By this time they had initiated a search party coming back from Camp IV and a party was being organized at Camp II to move up the glacier in an attempt to locate me. I raised Camp II on the radio and explained to Bill that I felt good and was having no problems.

Down at Camp II we were relieved to hear that Kiwi had reached Camp III and was safe inside his sleeping bag. We heard from Camp IV on the South Col that Dave Read was going to spend the evening there, sleeping on oxygen with the rest of the team, and the following day would stay at the camp, his stated objective. I was feeling disappointed to be back at Camp II. It was just a question of logistics and timing that now had me sitting there watching the summit attempt being made by others.

Meanwhile, at the South Col, as Laurie said later:

[The Sherpas] finally came back about eight o'clock . . . so then four of us were in the tent. . . . The stove never stopped, we just kept changing the cylinder, again and again, more tea, more tea, more tea, finally it was ten thirty. . . . I asked Sungdare, "What do you think?"

"Well," he said, "We can do it."

I said, "OK. I didn't sleep at all last night, and I won't get much sleep tonight."

He said, "One, two night—no sleep, ok."

I had talked to Dave before, I had said we had a problem. There wasn't enough oxygen for all of us to have insurance when we went up high. You know, for us to take two bottles. He'd said that if there was enough, he'd probably like to give it a go. . . . And I said, "Well, that would be all right if we had more, but I think we're

OVERLEAF
The view from the summit of Everest looking across Nuptse into the Himalayan range in Nepal.

174

gonna have troubles, because when we leave, we should leave with full bottles."

. . . . I think there were five full bottles left. So Dave thought about it and then said, "Well, it seems to me that you're the strongest, so I'll sit tight. I don't mind, I'm happy to have reached the South Col."

. . . . I finally got into my bag, and it was after 11 o'clock. . . . I put my oxygen set at two and took my boots out of my bag, and I took the liners out, and I stuck my mitts inside, and filled the thermos full of tea and had that inside my bag and had everything lined up, and a bit of tea left in the pot so I could just turn the stove on in the morning and there was enough for one cup. I got everything set up, pack all arranged, and we agreed to leave at 3:00. Slept good.

Woke up, mask all full of ice and everything, got ready, woke the Sherpas up. They were a bit slower getting up.

I was tired, but it's almost—it's almost like, it's not important. In order of priorities, this came so low on the list. This was the culmination of so much time and effort, so much of other people's sweat had led up to that moment, that being tired was low on the list. Unless it affected my judgement and that, and I just felt pumped, you know, I was full of adrenalin. . . . I wasn't terrified, but you know, I was a bit scared . . . I didn't know what was waiting up there.

I made sure my feet were really warm before I put my boots on and I put my crampons on inside the tent, and then I waited. Just waited, until they were ready, which was 4 o'clock or five after. I said goodbye to Dave and I pulled out. Helped them on with their oxygen, straightened it all out, got mine set up. . . .

And we left at 4:15. You know, all tied on. And then, damn! My foot was freezing. But we were moving fast and it was windy and it was cold, and I looked, but you know I couldn't walk and look at the same time because I had my oxygen mask on and my hood and it restricted my vision. . . . I had to stare down, so my hood would protect my face, and I would look up, briefly, and I couldn't get a perspective of where we were headed.

Now, all I knew was that we were on green ice. And I'm using the French technique and I'm looking at Lhakpa Dorje and he's not moving quite as smoothly as I'd like, and I looked at Sungdare and he's moving straight forward, not super technique, but just good, and solid. And I'm thinking, OK, no one's gonna fall, because if one of us falls that'll pull the other two guys off.

The pace was really getting to me, and I didn't want to crank my oxygen up . . . I thought I would overcome it with technique or pace . . . Sungdare was just boom, boom, boom going up the thing, and he said, turn it up. But I wasn't turning it up. I didn't want to, you see, because I thought, that's got to be the easy way out, there's gotta be another way of doing this without using so much oxygen, and I'm still going on a flow rate of two. . . .

Then we got to a place where we stopped, and there was enough light, and we sat down on a rock ledge. We'd passed the ice and everything, and we could see the sun rising in Tibet. A bit of light starting. We took our headlamps off and laid them on a rock. We rested there for three, four minutes and started off again.

Hell, it was *hard*. It was really hard. I just found it hard to keep up with Sungdare. . . . And that's when I noticed this mass up on my right-hand side, up on the rocks, that didn't seem to fit into the surroundings, and that was the dead woman. But I didn't know that, until we were really close to her. . . . Wow! Don't look back at her, try not to think about it. And when we got to 27,500, my foot was frozen. Couldn't feel a thing. I kept kicking it and trying to get some circulation. . . . Sungdare went and dug around for bottles, and I just took my mask off, then I took my boot off, gave them my Thermos. They drank the tea and kept offering me tea, but I couldn't warm my foot with both hands and drink tea at the same time. . . . I was thirsty as hell, but I wanted to get my foot going. That was more important. I warmed it for three or four minutes, put my sock back on, put my boot on, laced it not too tight, put my crampons on again.

Lhakpa Dorje started leading, but he was slower than Sungdare, so I kind of climbed up to him and then waited and waited and paced a bit . . . he was going one way and I could see it was easier going another way, so I went to show him where it was easier, and before long Sungdare just switched around because the guy wasn't moving fast enough. And then we started going up to the South Summit. And there the snow was breaking. It was harder for Sungdare because he was breaking trail. When I got to it, I'd just push the crust with my knees, just push my leg through. Poor old Lhakpa Dorje, with his short legs, he was having a hard time. Sungdare is tall for a Sherpa, about 5 feet 10 inches.

When I had trouble with the pace Sungdare would say, "Don't worry. Turn up the oxygen." I was worried about running out. But he'd say, "Don't worry. I got more."

Sungdare and Lhakpa
Dorje on the summit of
Everest with the Nepalese
flag. These two Sherpas
accompanied Laurie
Skreslet to the summit and
made a major contribution
to the success of the
expedition.

The view from the roof of
the world looking into
Tibet. Sherpa in the
foreground begins to
unpack Nepalese flag.

So we pushed to the South Summit. The views are fantastic. And every now and then, Sungdare would look at me, and I could see under his mask that he was grinning, and he'd say, "You're lucky!" That's about all he said between the South Col and the top— "You're lucky!" He meant about the weather. The wind wasn't so bad, the temperature wasn't so bad . . . it was cold, but we kept moving and we were all right. Within 20 minutes my foot had warmed up. So we pushed up to the South Summit, descended the other side, and then we could see the Main Summit.

And up till then, I still didn't know how far we had to go. I thought it was way further. I thought we were going to be eight or nine hours getting to the top. Sungdare figured we'd make it to the top at 10:30. At the very latest, 11:00. The ridge gave me a twinge of fear. I looked at the Hillary Step and it was *steep*, you know. Corniced on this side. I thought, we'd better not fall off *that!* We could climb it, I'm not worried about that, but we're roped together. It's not just me I'm thinking about. I've got to trust in the abilities of two guys. Lhakpa Dorje was a bit clumsy, you know, he didn't put his axe all the way in when he was moving, he'd move with his axe *out*, and he never kicked twice in steps.

Every time I put my axe in I thought, I'm not going to die on this because I made a stupid mistake. If I die because of a storm coming in or something, all right. Lack of judgement, that I just didn't have the experience to foresee, OK. But when it comes to putting my axe in, it goes right in to the head. And when it comes to putting my foot down, it's twice. Every time I put my foot in, I'd slide, with the edge of my blades, and then put my foot in, every time, because obviously I could move quicker than Sungdare, because he was kicking steps, but he'd just kick them enough to support him. I'd re-establish them and make them better. And then Lhakpa Dorje would come and step in them. But he would do funny things, like traverse with his axe out. And I kept saying, "Put it in your other hand," and sometimes he'd shift it around but even then in the wrong hand, and that made me wonder a bit. . . . God, I was hoping we weren't going to make any mistakes.

We got to the Hillary Step. I think any of us could have led it, although I don't think Lhakpa Dorje would have liked to, and poor Sungdare, his glasses kept fogging up . . . it was no big deal, you just had to be careful when you were pulling up on it. Sungdare just got up to it and sat down and snugged up a tight rope and brought me and Lhakpa Dorje up with six feet of rope between us.

From there, we set off, and kept moving, and there were a few places Sungdare would step up onto a slab and it would break off so I yelled at him, "Forget it, just go underneath them! Let's not take a chance of one of the things busting off!" One section he stepped on, cracked off, and just fell, but didn't slide. After that, Sungdare went low, around everything, going underneath these big slabs that were laying there like dinner plates, with the edges eroded under, two or three feet thick. So we weaved around those until we were in position to actually see the top. Son of a gun! There it was!

We plodded on up, and Sungdare climbed up to the top first, and let out a yell. I got up, put my axe on the hitch of the cornice at the top there, the main cornice is in Tibet on the right, but it's a ramp, you get to the top, it's a step, the final top. I went to step up and I broke through and fell to my knee, went to step up again, broke through, fell to my knee, put my axe in, pulled up, and just stood up on top.

Then Lhakpa Dorje came, stood up there, we congratulated each other, and they sat down, sort of looking around. I sort of stood by myself, looked around, tried to see everything. Just looking at Makalu. Looking *down* on Nuptse, that was a pleasure! . . . There was a sense of satisfaction looking down on a mountain that had defeated us two years before. Then we just stood around, taking photographs with my Leica, until all the film was shot. Then I pulled out the Minox, took some more, gave the Minox to them, and got them to take a few pictures of me.

I took all the pictures of them with the Nepalese flag with the Leica and they all turned out, all the Leica photographs turned out fine . . . the Minox is what froze up. And, well, you know, time whizzed by pretty quick. . . .

Laurie could see footsteps far below, on the West Ridge, where the Catalans were working. He noticed that the Chinese tripod that had prevailed for some years was now gone, perhaps buried. And he was also able to see what he thought must be the top of Polish Pillar (or Canadian Spur), and was happy that he was not on its rotten, unstable rock.

They had arrived at 9:30 a.m. It had taken them only five hours and 15 minutes to the reach the summit, a very good time. They left the summit just after 10:00. The Pilatus Porter airplane flew by, hoping to get video tape of them on the summit. It only managed, they learned later, to see the yellow oxygen bottle they had left on the summit.

"I wasn't deluding myself that I was any big Himalayan climber, Laurie said later. "I mean . . . I mean, it crossed by mind, 'This is something, eh? I got to the top of the world.' But the reality of it was I was lucky. The oxygen, weather, good Sherpas.''

Laurie still had energy and felt impatient that Lhakpa Dorje was too slow. He thought about unroping near the South Col, but just then, he slipped partway into a hidden crevasse. He got out, walked two feet, and went into another one. They were little crevasses, but it was still nice to be on a tight rope.

But as euphoria began to set in, he had to remind himself to be careful, that the summit climb wouldn't be a success until he got down alive. It was to easy to think, 'Hey, what are they gonna say back in Canada?' and stop paying attention to technique. He moved carefully, still putting the axe all the way in. It was too easy to get killed.

When they reached the tents, Dave met them with tea. Laurie asked if he'd been able to reach Camp II or Base Camp on the radio. Dave said he hadn't. But Laurie tried again, and they got through. He was just able to get the word out that they had reached the summit, and hear the congratulations and cheers. Then they realized their set wasn't transmitting any more.

That evening, when Laurie arrived at the base of the Lhotse face, Kiwi met him. He had congratulations from Laurie's girlfriend. Laurie couldn't believe it. The news had already reached Canada by telephone from Kathmandu, where they had received his summit message. Kiwi said that his girlfriend had a longer message, once Laurie could get to a radio.

Late that night, Laurie walked alone, over the even snow of the Western Cwm, under a full moon, and ran his girlfriend's words of love and support and happiness through his mind. He felt utterly drained, and very happy. It was only then that he could begin to contemplate the enormity of what he had done that day, and to sort out, as well as he could, all the thoughts and impressions that were starting to flood into his mind.

Al Burgess and Lhakpa Tshering above Camp IV with Makalu in the background. Tragically, Al's oxygen regulator froze and he was forced to abandon his summit bid at 27,500'.

Lhakpa Tshering and Pema Dorje on the summit with Laurie Skreslet's half empty oxygen bottle in the foreground.

On the summit ridge with the peak of Lhotse to the right of the climber's shoulder.

Pema Dorje on the summit of Everest.

KHURSAANI CHHA, OXYGEN CHHAINA*

THE FIRST SUMMIT was done, leaving us still with ropes and some equipment in place. Perhaps most important, we still had stable weather. Some were keen to get off the mountain, but others were ready for a second or even third summit attempt. Bill decided to hold things in place for at least one more push. It would be me, with Pema Dorje and Lhakpa Tshering.

*''If you eat chili, you don't need oxygen.'' —A Sherpa saying, advocating simplicity over technology.

The Sherpas were too tired to carry more oxygen and food back to the South Col, so all carries had to be done by the Western climbers.

Dwayne Congdon and Speedy Smith were to carry oxygen for my summit attempt, Lhakpa Tshering and Pema Dorje were to carry their own oxygen and Pat Morrow was to carry the video camera, taping the carries and activities at the South Col. Bill was going to take up a load for the New Zealand team. I was to use oxygen from Camp III in order to arrive rested at the South Col. In fact, everyone except Dwayne agreed to use oxygen above Camp III. The two Sherpas and I were to leave Camp II later than the others, so that we could, en route, add to our inventory any oxygen bottles that didn't make it all the way to the Col.

As we left Camp II, I could see Dwayne and Pat had already left Camp III and were beginning the traverse, 1,800 feet above us. When I arrived at Camp III, Speedy was already there, ready to move on up. I donned my oxygen equipment, carrying one bottle, and attempted to test out the diluted demand system I would be using the next day. I already had been almost to 26,000 feet (8000m) two days before without oxygen, so I did not expect to have any problems reaching the South Col with it. I passed Bill below the Yellow Band and caught up with Pat and Dwayne, who were a short distance above. Dwayne was struggling without oxygen under his load of two oxygen bottles. I took one of his bottles.

Even though I felt that my oxygen system was not fully operating, I quickly reached the Lhotse New Zealand Camp IV, 200 feet below the South Col. The last section was a little steeper, and I turned the dial on my oxygen system, anticipating the full flow. Something was not functioning properly however, and I was moving slower than I thought I should be. I had felt stronger before. Just as I pulled out onto the South Col and began the easy traverse to the tents, I looked down and realized that, instead of turning my oxygen to setting four, I had actually turned it down to setting one. For the last 200 feet I had been carrying two oxygen bottles and getting very little from them.

When I arrived at the box tent on the South Col, I checked my equipment. I saw by the pressure gauge that in fact I had used very little oxygen all day. That meant that the incorrect setting toward the end had only been apart of the problem. Reasonably satisfied with my perform-ance, I took off the encumbering oxygen set and set it down outside the tent. I had carried up a large adjustable wrench to use in a search around the South Col for more oxygen. If I could find two more bottles, one of the other climbers would be able to stay the night. Shortly after, the two Sherpas arrived. Lhakpa Tshering had even picked up a third oxygen bottle on the way. His feat of carrying almost 60 pounds at this elevation, even given the fact that he was using oxygen, was remarkable.

The weather was fine with very little wind. The summit seemed almost a foregone conclusion. As the Sherpas set about melting snow to make a drink, I searched around the Col and eventually found two or three half-empty bottles of oxygen and a couple of reasonably full ones. Now, if Dwayne Congdon arrived, we would have enough oxygen to support an extra member.

He did arrive; he had come all the way without oxygen. He had worked selflessly to support a second summit attempt. Even then, with his characteristic modesty and generosity, he stepped down so that Pat Morrow could stay and shoot video tape.

Dwayne wrote in his diary:

Personally, I felt that if I could get at least to the South Col without oxygen, that would be just as significant a mountaineering accomplishment *for me*, and I emphasize the *for me*, as it would be to get to the summit. . . . Certainly the summit is a great mountaineering accomplishment and I wanted it as much as anyone else. But I felt that in terms of my future career in high mountains . . . it was important to make the effort . . . to go to the South Col without gas . . . then the climber would hopefully have a better chance of surviving at extreme altitude.

Eventually it became apparent that there was enough gas for Al and two Sherpas to go, plus enough for either Pat or myself to go to the South Summit but probably no further. So one of us had to go down. As we discussed our situation, I got the strong feeling that logically I should go down and Pat should stay. Pat was a much better photographer than myself and he had carried up the video recorder so he could shoot some tapes, a definite priority of ours.

That evening I fastened an oxygen bottle onto my packframe and I was ready for tomorrow. I went to the box tent and sat inside with the two Sherpas, eating soup and noodles and drinking tea. We happily chatted. The Sherpas were quietly confident. When I told them I didn't want to be dragged up the mountain, they laughed and said, "You don't have to worry."

The political objectives of the expedition had been satisfied with the first summit ascent. I felt now that maybe we could do it in a little better style. I was tempted to try it without oxygen, or hoped that, if I used the dilute-demand system, I would only have to use one bottle. This would mean that we could climb faster, and I wouldn't have to take oxygen from the Sherpas. I wanted to feel that I was on equal terms with my Sherpa companions, not a client in the hands of guides.

I checked that the oxygen systems were working and that the Sherpas had half a bottle each to use through the night. They were using the constant-flow masks, which are the fail-safe masks. When I returned to my tent, I prepared my own sleeping oxygen. Pat was already laid out in his sleeping bag, with an oxygen bottle at his side and his constant-flow mask on his face.

I tried to use my dilute-demand mask for sleeping but, because of the need to suck deeply, I couldn't fall asleep. Each time I started to nod off I would begin to choke. So I sat up and got my headlamp working (flickering with a bad connection) and attempted to get the small, plastic sleeping mask to function. It had been crushed in a stuff sack. The plastic pipe was bent closed. I cut out the bend and re-inserted the pipe. By now it was dark and getting colder. Condensation was freezing on the mask, again shutting off the flow. After half an hour of frustration I gave up the effort to use the equipment. I made myself a good pillow, pulled the sleeping bag up around my head, and prepared to sleep without oxygen.

Through the night I had sensations of dreamy fatigue, the soft shaking of the tent fabric, and the lulling warmth of the sleeping bag. I don't think I ever fell into a deep sleep, but I wasn't having any problems. Now and again I would waken and think: I should be having problems, I have no oxygen! But there was no headache or feeling of sickness, so I just relaxed and enjoyed the rest.

At 3:00 a.m. the alarm went off. I shouted across to the Sherpa tent "Hey, Pema. Three o'clock. Put the water on." After five minutes of deep breathing I sat up, expecting to feel a throbbing headache. I was astonished that I didn't have one and in fact felt quite hungry. I seemed to be perfectly acclimatized!

The weather seemed good. I couldn't really tell in the darkness, but at least there was no wind. I climbed out of the tent and pulled on my boots and overboots. Even though I was wearing no down jacket over my Thinsulate suit, I felt quite warm. I went across to the Sherpa tent and climbed inside. The hanging stove in the middle of the tent simmered away, giving out a golden glow. I sat sideways across the tent, waiting for a breakfast of tsampa gruel. When this had cooked for a minute or two, Pema threw some powdered orange drink into it, to give it a sharp taste. He presented me with bowl after bowl of this mixture, saying, "The more you eat, the stronger you are." Two cups of tea followed and then I couldn't wait to get going.

At just past 5:00, we lifted the pack frames and oxygen bottles onto our shoulders. We roped up on a short rope. Lhakpa Tshering went first,

Lhakpa Tshering and Pema Dorje on the summit.

188

carrying two bottles of oxygen. Then me, with one bottle and the diluter-demand system. Third was Pema Dorje, also carrying two bottles, and at the end Pat Morrow, with two bottles and a constant-flow system. He intended to go as far as possible to take photographs.

We moved out very quickly at about 5:20 a.m. The ground was not too difficult to begin with, and we climbed upwards on undulating glacial ice until we eventually reached some hard snow. It was still dark and there was very little wind. I was feeling strong. My lungs were heaving, but then one expects a certain amount of difficulty above 26,000 feet.

The Sherpas were pressuring the rope for speed. I turned my oxygen up to setting three, but I didn't notice any improvement. Shortly after, Pat said that he would untie and proceed at his own speed. I didn't argue. After all, he was only going a little way up and could come down when he felt like it.

At 1,200 feet above the Col, just at daybreak, my attention was firmly on my breathing. I realized that I was beginning to suffocate. Suddenly, I ripped off the mask. Oxygen flooded into my lungs. I took off my pack frame and checked the pressure gauge. I hadn't used *any* oxygen! We'd been going for an hour and a half and I hadn't used any oxygen.

The diaphragm was frozen. I had been getting nothing but ambient air —and even that through a small aperture on the demand valve. It had been like breathing through a straw.

The two Sherpas waited, concerned, trying to figure out what was wrong with the system. It was too precarious a situation to take off gloves and dismantle such a delicate instrument. Pat caught up and moved past. He waited above on some broken rocks.

When Lhakpa Tshering realized that my oxygen system would not function, he said, "Al, I think you must take my oxygen." I looked up at him. I could tell by his expression that, as sincere as he was, he was suppressing a strong ambition to make the summit. I couldn't take his oxygen away from him.

Both Sherpas, after discussions with Bill, understood themselves to be part of the summit team, and had built all their hopes on a summit bid. Pema Dorje's face revealed his dilemma. He was an extremely motivated climber, perhaps even more than any of the Western climbers. He had also become a very close friend of mine. I realized that the only way I could get to the summit and satisfy my own ethics would be if I did it without oxygen, or if Pat Morrow were to offer me his. Even then, I wondered how happy I would be.

Lhakpa Tshering, in a fit of anger, said, "You must ask Pat." I realized that would commit Pat to a descent without oxygen. But I wavered. I thought, heck, I'm not having any trouble here. He should be able to go down all right! But he would have to make that offer. I couldn't ask him. If he volunteered, then he understood the responsibility for his own actions and would voluntarily go down without oxygen.

All these thoughts flashed through my mind. I was surprised at how rational I was, how rational I could be. I thought again: could I take oxygen from Lhakpa? No. How would I feel afterwards? No, I couldn't.

"You go on," I told them.

Lhakpa Tshering's eyes showed deep concern. "I never went there without a sahib."

"You must go. For yourselves," I said.

Lhakpa's confusion only deepened. Pema wavered, looking from me, up to Pat, and back again.

"Go to the summit. Both of you, for yourselves," I repeated.

Still undecided, both men slowly turned to face the slope. Suddenly, Lhakpa blurted out, in English, "Shit!" He booted his crampons in, plunged his axe, and started up, Pema following. I stood there for two or three minutes watching them move. They climbed so naturally and so quickly upwards. Those two deserved the summit.

I wondered again about trying without oxygen. We had come almost 1,200 feet in an hour and a half. I had been carrying the dead weight of an inoperative full bottle and system. I had been sucking ambient air through a restricted valve. The pace had been fast, even for oxygen. Could I now proceed without these handicaps? Maybe at least to the South Summit?

It was time for realism. The fact was, I had *already* used critical energy. My legs were leaden. It was now academic how far I might have gone without oxygen. Now, 1,200 feet up, it was too late. My attempt would only jeopardize that of the Sherpas. It was time to descend.

For some time, on the steeper section, the actual descent preoccupied me, but a welter of thoughts teased insistently at the edges of my consciousness. As I came onto easier terrain above the Col, I sat down and took some photographs. After that, I cramponed on, feeling calmer.

A long-ago conversation with Reinhold Messner, the famous Tyrolean climber, came to mind. He had asked me if I intended to go without oxygen on the Canadian climb. I had told him that the expedition was set up to use oxygen and therefore wouldn't be paced correctly to acclimatize an oxygenless climber. He just smiled, implying that it might be more possible than I thought. It was the first time I had even considered it. The first of many times.

As I plodded on toward the Col, I began to realize that from the start, it had been a matter of choices. I had chosen the Canadian expedition

High altitude Sherpa, Pema Dorje, twenty-four-years-old, on the summit of Everest. This was Pema's first major expedition and he proved to be a very strong, hardworking Sherpa who earned his place on the summit through his committment to the expedition.

The view looking down the southwest face of Everest into the Western Cwm.

Pat Morrow on the summit of Everest—the second Canadian to stand on the top of the world's highest mountain.

The view into Tibet from the summit, looking down onto the Rongbuk Moraine.

over the Lhotse climb because it was cheaper. On the final assault, I had chosen to use oxygen from Camp III to the South Col so that I would be more rested. If I had had the choice, I would have slept on oxygen. The next morning, I had had the opportunity to climb without oxygen, but chose to use it. Up until now, every choice I made had been the easiest alternative. It had taken me until the summit was beyond my reach without oxygen to make the right choice. The choice I could live with.

One by one, as I descended, I encountered the four New Zealanders. Two of them invited me on their Lhotse summit bid the next day. I thanked them but declined. I was too tired. I found that I was not able to discuss my real state of mind with them. My conclusions were positive, but abstract and difficult to explain, even to climbers as close to me as my brother and Paul Moores. Up near the summit, it had been *my* choice. And I had determined then that, if I couldn't climb a mountain without oxygen, I didn't deserve to climb it.

Later that day we heard that Pat Morrow had reached the summit at 11:30 a.m. and had got back down to the South Col at about 2:00 p.m. He and the Sherpas had a straightforward ascent, following the trail that Sungdare had broken two days before. The rope that Sungdare had fixed on the Hillary Step was still there and made the ascent a little more secure.

Later, I heard Pat's story. After we parted above the South Col, the Sherpas moved up to Pat and tied in. Pat took the lead, "gaining strength the higher I went." Their weather was perfect. Visibility was a hundred miles in every direction. "It was as though we were in a stationary airplane, peering down on the tops of cumulus clouds 8,000 feet below," he recalled.

Pat, like Laurie, suppressed his elation to concentrate on a safe descent, and it wasn't till he approached Camp II at nightfall that the excitement began to set in. He then lay happily sleepless for three nights, going over and over the lofty remoteness and grandeur of the scenes in his mind . . . scenes that he knew he had in his camera.

That evening on the Camp I radio we heard that the Lhotse team had made it above 27,000 feet but the weather was changing, the wind was increasing in velocity on the final ridge, and the summit couloir they were in was beginning to throw powder avalanches down towards them. Paul Moores got a touch of frostbite and had to retreat early. The rest finally had to give up as the weather worsened. We met them at Base Camp two days later. They were safe, but disappointed at not reaching the summit. There was an empty feeling everywhere. The expedition was over. For Speedy Smith and me, Base Camp had been our most permanent address in the last 12 months. When we left Base Camp, we felt we were leaving home.

During the next couple of days, yaks arrived with Sherpanis (Sherpa women) driving them. They were coming to collect all the equipment and take it back down to Lukla.

Everyone found his own way down in small groups, back down towards Lukla. From there, we would fly to Kathmandu.

On the morning of October 12, Peter Spear, Speedy, and I finished the packing of our personal equipment and set off down towards Lobuche. This was the first time I had seen grass since the middle of August, almost two months before. The smell of flowers and plants wafted up the valley. We were back to the easy life!

The first night back in Kathmandu, we attended a large cocktail party in the Sheraton Hotel. I hadn't seen so many people in a group for a couple of months. After the excitement and concentration of the climb, the idle chatter of a cocktail party was hard to adjust to. How can one convey to people in a modern hotel what it feels like to be way up at the end of a rope, climbing upwards in the frozen snow, with the sun bouncing off snow crystals and the wind whistling around your head, waves of spindrift everywhere, and the backdrop of the mountains dropping way down to the valleys? How can you describe all this?

The news media were mainly interested in Bill March as leader, and Pat Morrow and Laurie Skreslet as summit climbers. Most of the others kept out of the way. For some, this would be the last expedition. For others it would be a beginning. For me, it was just one step in a career. Maybe some day I'll go back to Everest. But there are fourteen 8,000-metre mountains—and I consider every one of them a challenge.

Pat Morrow giving the thumbs-up sign on the summit of Everest.

PERSONNEL

John Amatt

(business manager)

Aged 36, married with one child, living in Canmore, Alberta. Consulting Associate with The Banff Centre School of Management and Program Director for Banff Wilderness Seminars for business executives.

1965—Troll Wall, Norway, first ascent

1967—North Face of Sondre Trolltind, Norway, first ascent

1966—Nevado Alpamayo (19,512′) in Peru

Experience in Arctic Norway and Baffin Island

Orizaba (18,880′) in Mexico

Muztagata (24,757′) in China (summit attempt prevented by illness)

Tim Auger

(climber)

Aged 34, married with one child, living in Canmore, Alberta. Avalanche specialist for Banff National Park.

Numerous rock and ice ascents in North America

1977—Pumo Ri (23,442′), Nepal

Mt. Logan (19,850′) East Ridge, Yukon

Rusty Baillie

(climber)

Aged 41, married with two children, living in Calgary, Alberta. Instructor of Outdoor Pursuits, University of Calgary.

Number of European alpine routes

Eiger North Face

Brouillard, Right Hand Pillar (first ascent)

Sondre Trolltind North Face, Norway

Mount Kenya (17,040′), Kenya

Kilimanjaro (19,340′), Kenya

Cotopaxi (19,347′), Ecuador

Chimborazo (20,701′), Ecuador

Orizaba (18,880′), Mexico

Mt. Logan, East Ridge (19,850′), Yukon

Nuptse (25,850′), aborted after rockfall

Aconcagua (22,800′), Argentina. Retreated due to lack of equipment.

Stephen Bezruchka

(high altitude doctor)

Aged 38, married with one child, living in Seattle, Washington. Doctor in private practice.

1967—Tirich Mir (25,260′), Pakistan (unsuccessful)

Mt. Logan East Ridge (19,850′), Yukon

Muztagata (24,757′), China

James Blench

(climber)

Aged 26, single, living in Canmore, Alberta. Mountaineering Instructor.

Ice and alpine climbing in the Rockies

Gangapurna South Face (24,457'), Nepal

Al Burgess

(climber)

Aged 34, single, living in Calgary, Alberta. Professional mountaineer.

OVER 20 NORTH FACE ALPINE ROUTES IN EUROPE INCLUDING:

North Face of Triolet Direct (first British ascent)

Gletscherwand (first British ascent)

North Face, Grandes Jorasses (third ascent)

Central Pillar, Fresnay

Brouillard, Left Hand Pillar

North Face, Les Droites (second ascent)

Bonatti-Zappelli Eckpheiler Buttress (second ascent)

Numerous rock and ice climbs in North America

EXPEDITIONS:

South Face McKinley (20,320'), Alaska. First ascent alpine style

Southwest Buttress of Mt. Logan (19,520'). First ascent alpine style

Fitzroy, Patagonia

Huano Potosi (19,980'), Bolivia. Second ascent West Ridge

Huascaran Norte North Face (21,500'), Peru. Second ascent, first alpine

Ali Ratna Tibba (18,200'), India. First ascent West Face

1979 Annapurna II (26,040'). Failed at 23,000'. Alpine style

1980 Nanga Parbat (26,600'). Climbed Rupal Face to 24,500'. Failed to reach summit

1980–81 Everest West Ridge in winter. Failed at 24,000'

1981 Dhaulagiri I (26,810'). First Canadian 8,000 metre peak

1981–82 Annapurna IV winter (24,688')

Dwayne Congdon

(climber)

Aged 25, single, living in Calgary, Alberta. Mountaineering Instructor.

Ice and alpine routes in North America

Les Droites, North Face, French Alps

Grandes Jorasses, North Face, French Alps

Orizaba (18,800'), Mexico

1981 Gangapurna (24,457'). Retreated due to illness

1981 Nuptse (25,850'). Expedition aborted due to rock fall

Jim Elzinga

(climber)

Aged 27, single, living in Calgary, Alberta. Professional photographer.

Numerous alpine ascents in the Rockies

Kitchener North Face in winter

Cromwell North Face in winter

Slipstream (First ascent)

1979 Logan Southwest Buttress (19,520'), Yukon. (First ascent alpine style)

1981 Dhaulagiri I (26,810'). Retreated due to illness

1981 Nuptse (25,850'). Expedition aborted due to rock fall.

Kurt Fuhrich

(Base Camp cook)

Aged 33, single, living in Banff, Alberta. Chef and restaurant owner.

Mt. Kota Kinabalu (13,455'), Borneo

Mt. Damavand (18,386'), Iran

Lloyd "Kiwi" Gallagher

(deputy leader)

Aged 42, married with two children, living in Canmore, Alberta. Alpine Specialist for Kananaskis Provincial Park (Province of Alberta) with special responsibility for mountain rescue and public safety programs.

Alpine climbing in New Zealand and Canadian Rockies

Nevado Yerupaja (21,759'), Peru

Mount Logan (19,850'), Yukon

Pumo Ri (23,442'), Nepal

Muztagata (24,757'), China

Blair Griffiths [1949-1982]

(photography, video)

Resided in Vancouver, B.C. where he was employed by Abortel as a cameraman. Rock climbing and general mountaineering experience in the North Cascades and B.C. Coast Range, including some first ascents.

West rib on Mount McKinley

Cordilleia Blanca in Peru including Ranrapaika

David Jones

(Base Camp doctor)

Aged 50, married, living in Calgary, Alberta. Physician.

Expedition doctor on expeditions to Iceland, Greenland, Antarctica, and Nepal plus 34 years of civilian and military mountaineering experience.

Bill March

(expedition leader)

Aged 40, married with one child, living in Calgary, Alberta. Co-ordinator of the Outdoor Pursuits Program, Faculty of Physical Education, The University of Calgary, and an Instructor in Mountaineering.

Numerous ice and rock climbs in Europe and North America

1974 Dhaulagiri IV (25,135'). Aborted after three Sherpas killed

1979 Mt. Mera (21,300'), a trekking peak in Nepal

1981 Nuptse (25,850'). Retreated from 21,000' after advanced base camp was wiped out by rock fall

Chimborazo (20,701'), Ecuador

Cotopaxi (19,347'), Ecuador

Popocatepetl (17,600'), Mexico
Ixticcihuatl (17,400'), Mexico

Roger Marshall

(climber)

Aged 40, married with two children, living in Golden, British Columbia. Contractor and entrepreneur.

A number of European alpine climbs
Ice and rock climbs in North America
Mount McKinley South Face (20,320'), Alaska
Aconcagua (22,800'), Argentina
1981 Annapurna IV (24,688') winter

Dave McNabb

(climber)

Aged 26, married, living in Vancouver. Moutaineering Instructor.

Numerous alpine ascents in the Rockies
1981 Gangapurna (24,457'). Retreated due to illness
1981 Nuptse (25,850'). Expedition aborted due to rock fall.

Pat Morrow

(climber)

Aged 29, single, living in Kimberley, British Columbia. Freelance photographer.

Extensive ski touring in North America
Mt. McKinley (20,320'), Alaska
Aconcagua (22,800'), Argentina
Muztagata (24,757'), China

Bruce Patterson

(journalist)

Aged 32, married, living in Calgary, Alberta. Journalist.

Cotopaxi (19,437'), Ecuador

Dave Read

(climber)

Aged 33, single, living in Vancouver. Millwright.

Many alpine ascents in Europe and North America
Mt. McKinley (20,320'), Alaska
Aconcagua (22,800'), Argentina

Don Serl

(climber)

Aged 33, married, living in Vancouver Buyer for a mountain equipment co-operative.

Numerous alpine climbs in British Columbia
Mt. McKinley (20,320'), Alaska
Nevado Huascaran (22,205'), Peru
Ranrapallka (20,217'), Peru
1981 Annapurna IV (24,688'). Reached 21,050'

Laurie Skreslet

(climber)

Aged 32, single, living in Calgary. Mountain Guide.

Numerous ice climbs in the Rockies
Nevado Huascaran (22,205'), Peru
Nevado Chopikalki (20,817'), Peru
Nevado Kayesh (18,770'), Peru
1981 Nuptse (25,850'). Expedition aborted due to rock fall
Aconcagua (22,800'), Argentina. Retreated due to lack of equipment

Gordon ''Speedy'' Smith

(climber)

Aged 36, single, living in Calgary. Mechanical engineer.

Extensive alpine climbing in Europe and North America
1974 Pik Lenin (23,406'), Russia. Alpine style
Aconcagua (22,800'), Argentina
1981 Annapurna IV (24,688') winter. Retreated at 23,000'

Peter Spear

(Base Camp manager)

Aged 41, married with two children, living in Calgary, Alberta. Teacher and education administrator.

Numerous alpine ascents in the Canadian Rockies
Nevado Huascaran (22,205'), Peru
Nevado Pisco (18,898'), Peru
Akilpo Sur (18,242'), Peru
Nevado Paqtsasuri (17,471'), Peru

ACKNOWLEDGEMENTS

Space prohibits the acknowledgement of the hundreds of companies and the thousands of individuals, all of whom made indispensible contributions to the success of The 1982 Canadian Mount Everest Expedition, sponsored by Air Canada. They are all a part of the exceptional "team" who contributed to the first Canadian ascent of the world's highest mountain, and our heartfelt thanks go out to all of them.

The following, therefore, is but a short list of the major contributors.

Canadian Mount Everest Society
Patron
Rt. Hon. Roland Michener, P.C. Q.C.

Officers
President
Mr. Roy Fisher

Vice-President
Mr. Bill March

Secretary
Mr. Mike Simpson

Treasurer
Mr. Peter Simpson

Directors
Mr. Sandy Fitch
Mr. Lloyd Gallagher
Mr. Helmut Microys
Mr. Gordon Smith
Mr. Jay Straith

Business Manager
Mr. John Amatt

Associates
Sponsor Representative
Mr. Mike Breckon

Business Agent
Mr. Nevil Pike

Communications Consultant
Mr. Peter Hollidge

Expedition Agent in Nepal
Mr. Bobby Chettri

Major Financial Contributors
Aberford Resources Ltd.
Adeco Drilling & Engineering Co. Ltd.
Air Canada
Alberta Natural Gas Co. Ltd.
Banff Crag & Canyon Ltd.
Brass Craft Canada Ltd.
Cohos, Evamy & Partners
Consolidated Electric Distributors Ltd.
Dynamic Drilling Fluids Ltd.
East Hills Chrysler Plymouth Inc.
Faster Oilfied Services Ltd.
Flint Engineering & Construction Ltd.
Genstar Ltd.
Government of the Province of Alberta
Investors Mortgage Corporation Ltd.
Jackman Foundation
John Labatt Ltd.

Kindred Industries
Knowlton Realty Ltd.
Lavalin Services Ltd.
Lincoln McKay Development
   Co. Ltd.
Lochiel Explorations Ltd.
Marline Oil Corporation
S.T. Fitch
Simmons Drilling Ltd.
The Royal Bank of Canada
Toronto Dominion Bank
Twin Lakes Secondary School
Western Breeders Ltd.

Equipment Suppliers

Acme Stamp Distributors Ltd.
   Marking devices
Adidas (Canada) Ltd.
   Running shoes and clothes
Alcan Aluminium Ltd.
   Ladders, tent frames, stakes
Austria Imports
   Wool mitts
Bausch & Lomb Canada Inc.
   Climbing glasses
B.D. Wait Co. Ltd.
   Heating and Lighting Equipment
Berghaus
   Yeti gaiters
Bic Inc.
   Lighters
Block Heater Head Wear
   Wool hats
Blue Water Ltd.
   Rope
Bon Del
   Water purifying equipment
L.F. Burgess & Associates
   Stoves, thermal clothing
Burlington Hosiery
   Socks
Canadian ABC Company
   Mountaineering skis
Canadian Mountain Supply
   Climbing harnesses
Canadian Mountaineering
   Equipment Ltd.
   Climbing packs

Cascade Toboggan Rescue
   Equipment Inc.
   Rescue Toboggan
Chouinard Equipment Ltd.
   Climbing hardware, crampons
CP Sport Inc.
   Inner soles
Damart Thermolactyl Ltd.
   Mitten and glove liners
Domtar Packaging
   Packing boxes
Eddie Bauer Inc.
   Down underwear
ETS Petzl
   Ascendeurs, headlamps, helmets
Fergusson Atlantic
   Shirts
Forrest Mountaineering
   Ice axes
Forty Below Ltd.
   Neoprene Overboots
Fox River Mills Inc.
   Wool gloves
Genfoot Inc.
   Base Camp boots
Gillette Canada Ltd.
   Gas lighters
Gilmour Sports Ltd.
   Climbing boots
Gourock Industries Ltd.
   Polypropylene rope
Great Canadian Underwear
   Co. Ltd.
   Moisture absorbent socks
Hanson-Mohawk Inc.
   Wool socks
Helly-Hansen (Canada) Ltd.
   Pile clothing
Hitachi Denshi, Ltd. (Canada)
   Communications equipment
Howe & Bainbridge Inc.
   Klimate fabric
Johnson Diversified Canada Inc.
   Tents, packs, pack frames
Kodak Canada Inc.
   Photographic film
LSP Leader Sport Products
   Ski goggles

Life Support Engineering Ltd.
   Oxygen equipment
Manulux Corporation
   Ski goggles, jackets
North American Strong Box Corp.
   Aluminum packing boxes
Northsport Ltd.
   Polypropylene underwear
Power Conversion Inc.
   Lithium batteries
Republic Packaging Ltd.
   Foam mattresses
S.C. Johnson & Son Ltd.
   Hotshots
Simpson-Sears Ltd.
   Tool kits
Smico Inc.
   Swiss Army knives
Solar Cells Ltd.
   Solar charging panels
Sun Ice Ltd.
   Climbing clothing
Sybron Canada Ltd.
   Waterbottles, flashlights
3M Canada Inc.
   Thinsulate material
Teleglobe Canada
   Communications equipment
The Canadian Coleman Co. Ltd.
   Lanterns, ovens, sleeping bags, packs
The North Face
   Tents
Therm-A-Rest
   Air mattresses
Timex Canada Inc.
   Watches
Toronto Stamp Inc.
   Marking devices
Union Carbide Canada Ltd.
   Flashlights, batteries, plastic bags
Uptown Sewing
   Carmen gaiters
Western Rock Bit Co. Ltd.
   Propane cylinders
Westwood Pharmaceuticals
   Face and lip cream
Wild Leitz Canada Ltd.
   Cameras, binoculars

Woods Inc.
Tents, sleeping bags, down jackets
Wrangler
Jeans

Food suppliers
Alberta Sugar
Syrup
Ashner Food Products Ltd.
Packaging
B.C. Packers
Canned seafood
Bridge Brand Food Services Ltd.
Miscellaneous
Brooke Bond Inc. Ltd.
Oxo cubes, cheese, tea
C.E. Jamieson & Co. (Dominion)
Ltd.
Vitamins
Cadbury Schweppes Powell Inc.
Chocolate bars
Canada Packers Ltd.
Canned meats
Canada Starch Co. Ltd.
Packaged soups
Christie Brown & Co. Ltd.
Biscuits
Club House Foods Inc.
Spices
Domtar Chemicals Group
Salt
E.D. Smith & Sons Ltd.
Jams, sauces
Eddy Match Co. Ltd.
Matches
Food World Sales Ltd.
Powdered eggs
General Foods Inc.
Jello, Tang
General Mills Canada Ltd.
Granola bars
Harmony Orchards Ltd.
Herbal tea
H.J. Heinz Co. of Canada Ltd.
Sauces
Interbake Foods Ltd.
Biscuits

Kimberly-Clark of Canada Ltd.
Paper towels, toilet paper
Magic Pantry Foods Inc.
Foil-packed foods
Maple Leaf Mills Ltd.
Flour
McGavin Foods Ltd.
Fruit cake, Christmas pudding
MRB Sales
Popcorn
Nabisco Brands Ltd.
Fleichmann's Margarine, yeast
National Importers Ltd.
Chutney
Nestle (Canada) Ltd.
Hot chocolate, coffee, cheese
O'Connor Galloway
Candies
Proctor & Gamble Inc.
Cake mixes, soap, toothpaste
Quaker Oats Co. of Canada Ltd.
Porridge, pancake mixes
R.B. Hayhoe Foods Co.
Coffee
Reckitt & Coleman Canada Inc.
Mustard
Rowntree Mackintosh Canada Ltd.
Candies, chocolate bars
Seagrams Distilleries Ltd.
Alcoholic beverages
St. Lawrence Starch Co. Ltd.
Syrup, corn oil
Sunney Boy Ltd.
Instant porridge
The Continental Group of Canada
Canning of food
Thomas J. Lipton Ltd.
Canned meats, rice, tea
United Biscuits (Canada) Ltd.
Biscuits

Other Supporters
ATCO Group Services
Warehouse storage
Calgary Board of Education
Packing and storage space
Chubb Insurance Co. of Canada
Medical and life insurance

Cronkhite Companies Ltd.
Vehicle loan
Kentwood Ford Sales Ltd.
Vehicle loan
Mini-Drive Car Rental
Vehicle loan
Mullen Trucking Ltd.
Truck transportation
Raymond & Company Insurance
Agencies Ltd.
Insurance
Sheraton Hotels Worldwide
Hotel accommodation
The Banff Centre for Continuing
Education
Office support
The University of Calgary
Office support

APPENDIX I:

EXPEDITION FOOD

Kiwi Gallagher with Peter Spear

"What has 120 legs, and thrives on steep terrain at high altitude?"

Problem

Organize 9 tons of food (72 days × 60 people). Package and transport it 12,500 miles; make it tasty and nutritious, appealing to everyone's taste; provide a high calorie content. The food should be cheap, weigh little, and be able to be cooked under primitive conditions.

Solution

I realized at once that it was a vain hope to please everybody with a limited menu. Still, I circulated a proposed menu to the team members, and invited their comments. I got just three answers. Armed with these and a wealth of knowledge from my Pumori climb, I attacked the problem with zeal.

Approach March/Base Camp

On the approach march and at Base Camp the 4½ pounds per man per day allowance would consist of non-perishable foods from Canada, supplemented, where possible, by "local" food. The local food was mostly rice, lentils, eggs, potatoes, and fruit. Our packaged foods from Canada included soups, dry cereals, fruit, nuts, candy bars, powdered drink mixes, and "Magic Pantry" menus.

High Altitude

I felt that a drastic change in diet at high altitude could impair our physical condition and subsequent performance on the mountian. I therefore tried to maintain, as much as possible, the diet we had become accustomed to, while at the same time accommodating the body's changing needs at higher elevations. High calorie and liquid intake are essential at higher elevations. Four quarts of liquid a day are needed to combat dehydration, and a climber weighing 160 pounds and carrying a 40 pound load burns up approximately 3000 calories a day. With all these things in mind, the following sample menu was proposed.

Breakfast

Hot chocolate, porridge with brown sugar, biscuits with jam or honey, fruit.

Lunch

Chocolate, nuts, raisins, dried fruit, etc. Tang for throughout the day, candies, chocolate bars. Hot drinks with biscuits or fruit cake, Swiss Knorr instant soup mixes.

Evening meal

Magic Pantry entrees (eg. stew), mashed potatoes, peas, Christmas pudding, milk, tea, fruit cake. Approximate weight: 2½ pounds per man per day

Ten menus from Magic Pantry were available. Their lightweight, vacuum-sealed pouches contained precooked foods and were convenient to cook. The pouches needed only to be plunged into boiling water for several minutes to reheat the contents and the same water could then be used for drinking. This reduced fuel consumption, and further, the food could be eaten directly from the pouch, eliminating clean-up.

Once the amounts and kinds of food were determined, we turned our attention to the problem of packaging. Domtar Packaging donated all the boxes needed. Especially water-proofed with a plastic liner and made to accommodate a 60 pound load, the 600 boxes withstood the extensive man-handling and travel both to and on the mountain.

The mammoth task of ordering, receiving, weighing, and packing the food was then passed over to Peter Spear, the Base Camp manager, and Gordon Smith.

Gordon Smith spent about two weeks contacting suppliers to ascertain whether they handled the products needed. He then attempted to convince the supplier to donate the products to the expedition or provide them at cost. Jennifer Dean in the CanEverEx office in Toronto also was able to obtain donated food from major Canadian food suppliers with headquarters in the Toronto-Montreal area. Food products not obtained through Gordon or Jennifer were ordered through Gary

Wolfe and Val Procis at Bridge Brand Food Services in Calgary, at reasonable cost and usually within 24 hours.

This massive mound of food was accumulated over a six-week period in a staff lunch room in the basement of Queen Elizabeth Jr.–Sr. High School in Calgary. Jack Holt, the principal at Queen Elizabeth, had given his approval for food storage in the basement of the school, and the use of the cafeteria area for food packaging during the evenings and on weekends. Peter was the vice principal at Queen Elizabeth, and he was able to receive and inventory food items as they arrived. The room was 23 feet × 30 feet and filled five feet deep with cases of food. Tiny aisles were left to move products in and out of their areas as needed.

The packaging of the food seemed at first like an overwhelming task. The 1975 British Everest expedition had had a commercial packaging company put together all the food menus, and then package and label them. Over a period of 25 days, Peter, Cy Goddard, expedition members, school students, and many of Peter's friends and ski patrol buddies spent 800 hours of time in prepackaging and packing food. The packing sessions ran from 7:30 to 10:30 most evenings between March 15 and April 9, including weekends.

There were 18 different menus to assemble, plus two different types of kitchen supply boxes. Since products such as sugar, coffee, powdered milk, porridge, and tea were needed in different quantities at Base Camp, Camp II and above Camp II, a tremendous amount of prepackaging was necessary before menus could be assembled. During most evenings,

about 200 cubic feet of original boxes and wrappings were discarded. Sugar was repackaged by weighing the amount of sugar necessary, putting it in a milk shake container, and then trimming the container down to the level of the sugar, so an exact volume scoop could then be used to speed up packaging. Even cookies were repackaged and "high-tech packed" into ligher-weight plastic bags closed with twist-ties. Syrup and HP sauce were poured into plastic bottles. Brian Cougal brought his home canner to the school and, over a three-night period, canned over 300 pounds of margarine and 800 pounds of various types of nuts and mountain mix, with excellent results.

Menus were assembled from Kiwi's original list, and handled in three major groupings. The six approach march and Base Camp menus were lettered A-B-C-D-E-F and consisted of 66 pound boxes, each containing six separate 11 pound boxes to simplify packaging and protect food from damage. Camp I and II menus were lettered G-H-I-J-K-L and consisted of 44 pound boxes with four 11 pound boxes inside. Camp III-IV-V menus were lettered M-N-O-P-Q-R and each consisted of an 11 pound box, enough food for four climbers for three daily meals. Four different menu boxes were put into a 44 pound box for transport to Camp II, where they could be taken out of the larger box and transported individually to the designated camp. The kitchen supply boxes weighed 66 pounds for Base Camp and 44 pounds for Camp II.

Assembling each separate menu was a carefully co-ordinated project. For a Base Camp menu weighing 66 pounds, all the necessary items, in the proper quantities, had to be assembled. This food pile was then distributed equally into 6 smaller 11 pound boxes. Each small box was then labelled appropriately (eg. C1-C2-C3-C4-C5-C6) and a list of the contents of each box was typed and duplicated. Each small box was put at the head of a long chain of tables containing 11 pound boxes in the correct numbers. (Menu C alone had to be done 18 times.) The sample box was unloaded. Food packers would obtain materials from the store room and duplicate the sample the appropriate number of times, placing the food on the table in front of the boxes to be filled. When all the foods were in place, a plastic "kitchen-catcher" was put inside the 11 pound box, the food placed inside the bagged box, and twist ties added to seal the bag. Then the box was closed and taped shut.

When the appropriate number of boxes for a menu were finished, they were assembled into the larger, outer box. A 6 mm plastic bag was placed inside the outer box, and the 11 pound boxes were inserted. The plastic bags were then closed with a twist tie. The menu sheet for the contents of the large box was folded, placed inside a self-adhesive packing envelope attached to the lid of the box, and then the large box was stapled shut. The stapled seam was covered with two layers of 2 inch wide tape, making a good waterproof seal. Two ½ inch wide plastic straps encircled the box and were tightened through plastic buckles. The strapping was strong enough that the boxes could be lifted using the straps as handholds.

Next, the boxes were labelled with liquid-paint pens, using three codes on each box to ascertain the expedition sequence number, the eventual destination camp, and the menu/menus inside. For example, a box labelled 091-2-K indicated box 91 for Camp II and it contained the K menu. All boxes going above Base Camp also had coloured tape on diagonally opposite corners to ease sorting. A white taped box went to Camp I, yellow to II, green to III, blue to IV and red to V, although menus for Camps III, IV, and V were interchangeable.

The food prepackaging and packing techniques proved successful. Only one box suffered major damage, when a plastic container leaked syrup. The small 11 pound boxes provided internal strength for the larger boxes so there was usually only minor food damage such as a few crumbled cookies. Even the chocolate bars survived the heat of India and the three month storage at Khunde very well.

The food was flown in an Air Canada cargo plane from Calgary on April 16, along with the rest of the expedition gear. After landing at New Delih, the gear was trucked to Kathmandu. From there 10½ Twin-Otter loads of climbing clothing and expedition gear were flown to Lukla and stored at Khunde with the gear and food that was trekked in from Lamosangu. Some Base Camp gear was stored at Pheriche. In early August, Peter and Dave McNab arrived at Khunde and sorted the expedition gear into four different priority piles. These piles were later yakked and portered into Base Camp with two days between priority loads. This allowed time to assemble Base Camp and sort gear easily.

The food packing system had its strengths and weaknesses. Canning the nuts and margarine worked well, with no spoilage occurring. The Magic Pantry food was easy to prepare and was in sufficient variety, although we did not take enough fruit. Sending the food in pre-monsoon was a great advantage, since it was then stored only three days from Base Camp. Prepackaged menus were handy for the Sherpa cooks. The flattened cardboard boxes served as excellent insulation under tents in Base Camp. Although food was packed in Canada for the approach and return from Base Camp, the climb strategy later changed, resulting in surplus food. Base Camp food boxes were intended for climbers and Sherpas, but in fact, little food was used by the Sherpas so another surplus accumulated. Baking powder biscuits and the occasional loaf of bread were the baking successes. However, in spite of the adequate food, most climbers seemed to lose 20 pounds or more.

Considering that it was our first attempt at food packaging on this scale, things went well, thanks to many hours of volunteer workers, good planning techniques, and proper packaging facilities.

APPENDIX II

CLIMBING EQUIPMENT

Gordon Smith

Personal Equipment

No differentiation was made between ice fall and high-altitude Sherpas on this expedition. Wherever possible, all Sherpas were issued with the same equipment as the climbing members. The only personnel to be issued with substantially less equipment were the Base Camp staff and mail runners.

For the walk-in to Base Camp, Adidas (Canada) Ltd. generously provided us with a variety of clothing to keep us warm and comfortable during the 160-mile journey. Their excellent nylon shorts were used continually by every member of the expedition. Matching tops weren't so popular, because of size discrepancy. Nylon sweat suits were used on colder days, and their running shoes were comfortable enough for the long journey, most of it following stony trails. They did not, however, prevent leeches from crawling through the lace holes and sucking blood out of one's feet, so some members preferred a stouter hiking boot. The lightweight waterproof jacket and pants actually did work in the rain, although for deluges an umbrella was essential. Ordinary wool and cotton socks were provided for the walk-in by Burlington Hosiery and, again, survived the expedition without wearing out.

Camp Trails packs were provided by Johnson Diversified Canada Ltd. to carry the bulk of our personal equipment to Base Camp. These were excellent, roomy backpacks, fully adjustable to suit any size of person and easily accommodating all our belongings. However, our belongings were many and heavy, so these packs were carried for us by Nepali porters, whilst the pampered team members carried the few items required on the walk-in in Lowe Latok packs, provided by Canadian Mountaineering Equipment Ltd. These special climbing packs, also fully adjustable, were used without

exception by the team on the mountain. Portable tape recorders were donated by Hitachi Denshi (Canada) for personal entertainment on the journey. They had a record capability, and were used to record personal diaries, etc. Leica Minox cameras were also donated by Wild Leitz Canada Ltd. to every member of the team, and more sophisticated R4s and MP4s were lent to the members capable of handling them. Film was donated by Kodak Canada Inc.

For wandering through the slush and puddles around Base Camp, Genfoot Inc. donated waterproof and insulated boots. This popular boot, worn by the Canadian workman every day through our long winters, was very practical.

On the hill itself, the multi-layer system of clothing was used with great success. Warm and comfortable Lifa polypropylene underwear was donated by Northsport Ltd. Perspiration could pass through this material, leaving it dry and warm, and was collected in the next layer of clothing, a pile suit generously donated by Helly-Hansen (Canada) Ltd. This warm, light, comfortable but hard-wearing material has revolutionized clothing concepts in mountaineering over the last 12 years. Sherpas were provided with a two-piece suit of Helly-Hansen, since they preferred this style. (This had more to do with the relatively higher second-hand values of two-piece as compared to single suits, rather than any practical advantages.) Additional jackets were also donated to go over the suit for added insulation. Helly-Hansen mitts and socks were also donated to all members of the expedition. The socks were very warm and comfort-

able too, having no ribbed patterns to press into your feet. The gloves have the advantage of being very pliable—an important consideration when working in sub-zero temperatures.

Outer protective clothing was generously provided by Sun Ice Ltd. of Calgary for use low on the mountain. Mountain parkas and wind pants were specially made out of grey and red "Klimate". These excellently made garments were of such high quality that they made me feel self-conscious. For once in my life I was fashionable! The Klimate material was excellent in combatting wind and snow; unfortunately on the walk-in it had little effect in combatting the monsoon downpours. For wear higher up on the mountain, a made-to-measure high-altitude suit was produced for each climber.

The suit was made out of Thinsulite donated by 3M Canada Ltd. and covered by lightweight 2-oz. nylon. A full-length zipper up the front and both sides gave easy access and ventilation possibilities, extra reinforcing was added to the knees and backside, the hood was reinforced with a wire at the front to prevent it from flopping over the eyes, and a generous allowance was made to accomodate additional down clothing underneath and also the oxygen breathing mask. One small problem was the lack of provision of a half-moon "bomb door" in the back to facilitate answering the calls of nature. This was entirely our fault, as Sun Ice was not to know that the Helly-Hansen suits worn underneath were already equipped like that. Sun Ice also provided us with excellent insulated mitts (Thinsulite and Gortex) and

Klimate overmitts, as well as a very smart team jacket. The Sherpas were given insulated salopettes instead of these suits, also made by Sun Ice. In conjunction with this, a pair of Wrangler jeans was also donated by Work Wearhouse of Calgary.

Eddie Bauer Inc. donated down pants and jackets for wear under the high-altitude suits in super-cold conditions. This lightweight down clothing was excellently made and very popular for wearing in camp on cold days and nights. Koflach Ultra Extreme climbing boots were provided by Gilmour Sports Ltd., along with Alveolite inners. What can you say about the best high-altitude boot in the world? They were light, warm, and comfortable; the best endorsement is that we didn't have a single case of frostbite on the expedition.

Two types of gaiter were used, Yeti gaiters by Berghaus and Carmen by Uptown Sewing. Yeti were more popular because they covered the whole boot, but the rubber gasket split on occasion and the gaiter flipped up above the toe. Carmen gaiters were simpler and more traditional, just hooking on the bootlace, and were excellently made. However, they were too narrow to fit over double boots and even small climbers needed the extra large size to get the width right and then they were too long! For higher up on the mountain, neoprene overboots by Forty Below Ltd. were used. Inner soles were donated by CP Sport Inc. for use in our boots where necessary. We were also provided with many pairs of gloves: the popular Dachsteins from Austria Imports were used all over the mountain. Damart glove liners were donated by Damart Thermolactyl Ltd., and these were very useful for wear under mitts and for intricate work such as taking photographs. Woolen work gloves from Fox River Mills Inc. were also widely used. Fergusson Atlantic provided us with Duofold shirts, which were very popular, and L. F. Burgess and Associates provided us with Peter Storm Thermal Shirts, which unfortunately were a little tight on us, as well as more socks. Woolen socks were also supplied by Hanson-Mohawk Inc.

To keep our heads warm, ski toques were donated by Block Heater Head Wear. These were very popular with the Sherpas and around camp, but some climbers preferred the more traditional balaclava while actually climbing. For eye protection, Bausch and Lomb Canada Inc. donated glacier glasses which were used only on the lower part of the mountain. On the higher slopes, because of the continually cold winds, everybody preferred the additional protection of goggles. Both Bolle goggles donated by Manulux Corporation and Ultra Pro goggles donated by LSP Leader Sport Products were used. Manulux Corporation also donated Francital jackets, which were used for work in the ice fall and for wear around Base Camp in stormy weather. They also donated Chapsticks, which were excellent in preventing cracked lips all the way up the mountain. Presun Face and Lip Cream was donated by Westwood Pharmaceuticals to keep our faces and lips from blistering in the intense sun. Timex Solid State LCD watches were provided by Timex Canada Inc. and proved to be very reliable, the peace at Base Camp being shattered daily by the many renderings of "Aura Lee" from 30 to 40 wrist watch alarms!

A comprehensive version of the popular Swiss Army knife — Mountaineer model—was donated to all members of the expedition by Smico Ltd.

Johnson Diversified Canada Ltd. donated lightweight "Freighter" pack frames to the expedition. These were more popular with the Sherpas than ordinary packs and were excellent for carrying heavy objects like oxygen bottles and drums of rope between camps. The Canadian Coleman Co. donated some backpacks that were used by the Sherpas for ferrying loads between camps, as well as Hollow-Fill sleeping bags, which were used as spare bags by climbers returning to Base Camp from higher camps without sleeping bags. These bags were extremely warm and were coveted by the Sherpas, to whom they were given away as perks at the end of the expedition.

Down sleeping bags and parkas were especially made for us by Woods Inc. of Toronto. Woods' contribution to the success of our expedition was second only to Air Canada. The sleeping bags were roomy enough to climb into fully dressed if necessary and generously filled with down so that they were exceptionally warm. They had full-length zippers with a Velcro flap at the top to prevent the zipper from coming undone accidentally. The bags had Klimate outer coverings to protect them against the effects of melting hoar frost. The parkas were equally luxurious items, generously filled with down to be warm enough on the coldest day on the mountain. Hoods were large enough to pull over helmets if necessary, and once again, an allowance was made for an oxygen mask. Large pockets were provided, both on the inside and the outside of the jacket. Woods also donated an overbag which was made out of Thinsulite and covered in Klimate, also with a full-length zipper, which could be used over the down sleeping bag, or separately, on the walk-in. Bivouac bags were also made for each climber, in case of an involuntary night out, but thankfully were never used.

A variety of T-shirts was also provided for the expedition, some with team logos, some donated by the Alpine Club of Canada, and some from Mountain Travel of Nepal.

Climbing Equipment

With the exception of the ladder sections needed to bridge the crevasses in the Khumbu Ice Fall, every other item of climbing equipment tended to the standard.

The 8-foot aluminum ladder sections were generously supplied and modified by Alcan Aluminium Ltd. Extension pieces were bolted onto one end of each section to allow two or more sections to be slotted together to bridge wide crevasses. Pins retained by steel cables could then be slotted through the extensions to prevent the extensions from coming apart. Holes were drilled at either end and in the middle of the ladder sections to enable aluminum stanchions to be bolted on, to hold hand rails. Further, stabilizers could be bolted on underneath the ladder and tensioned with some steel cables to prevent the ladders from sagging while they were being crossed. Snow stakes were originally made

by Alcan, but these proved to be unsuitable. Alcan also made all our deadmen or snow flukes—used to anchor fixed ropes on the mountain. The swagging of the steel cables onto the deadmen was kindly done at short notice by Dick Howe in Calgary. He also pressed copper bushes through the holes in the aluminum ladder rungs to prevent the rope from being cut on the sharp holes. In the end, simple, effective, and lightweight aluminum snow stakes were made at short notice by Bruno's Sheet Metal of Calgary.

Littlejohn climbing harnesses and gear and hammer holsters were supplied by Canadian Mountain Supplics. The harnesses had the advantage of full adjustment between summer rock climbing with almost no clothes on and Himalayan mountaineering with bulky down on. However, they were rather complicated to put on. Ascenders, headlamps, and helmets were supplied by ETS Petzl. The ascenders were the most comfortable I have used with big mitts on my hands, but they had a tendency to slip with fresh snow on the rope. The excellent headlamps were modified to use with a Radio Shack battery holder and a long-running lithium D cell battery supplied by Power Conversion Inc. The helmets were provided for the Sherpas only, while the members took their own. Similarly, ice-axes were supplied for the Sherpas only, by Forrest Mountaineering. Climbers provided their own, most favouring a longer model. Specialist ice hammers and figure-of-eights were also provided by each climber, depending upon personal preferences. Carabiners, pulleys, pitons, ice screws, crampons, and straps were all supplied by

Chouinard Equipment Ltd.

Fixed and climbing ropes were supplied by Blue Water Ltd., and a lighter-duty ⅜-inch diameter polypropylene fixed rope for use in the icefall was donated by Gourock Industries Ltd. Miscellaneous items were also supplied by Prairie 'n' Peak, Mountain Equipment Co-op, and the Hostel Shop, all Calgarian equipment suppliers.

Tents

Many types of tents were used on Mount Everest, from huge frame tents used for mess and cooking tents at Base Camp, to the highly specialized box tents for use on the face. Johnson Diversified Canada Inc. generously donated Mushroom and Sentinel tents, which were used without problems at Base Camp and Camp I as personal tents. North Star tents were also used at Base Camp and advanced Base Camp as personal tents—these were very roomy and wind-resistant tents. Our own Santa Claus, Woods Inc., provided us with a wide range of tents, which were used from Base Camp to Camp IV on the South Col. A huge Prospector tent was used successfully as an eating tent at Base Camp for the entire expedition, despite the enormous weight of fresh snow regularly deposited upon it. Sportsman tents were used at Base Camp as a medical tent and communal housing for the Sherpas. They were used as cook tents at Camp I and advanced Base Camp (Camp II), until the winds got so strong that one blew away (anchored in a 60 mph wind, like a kite, by a climbing rope tied to a huge boulder). Eldorado tents were used at Base Camp as personal tents; Woods' excellent Dome tents—the most popular tents on the expedition —were used at Camps I, II, and IV. They were comfortable with two people and gear installed, and easily resisted the high winds to which we were regularly subjected. For some reason unknown to me, they featured a Gortex flysheet. Some J tents were also donated and used at Base Camp, Camps I, II and borrowed by the New Zealand team for use at their Camp IV at 26,000 feet. They also resisted the wind very well.

Probably Woods' *pièce de résistance* was their box tent. Despite a very complicated design (not Woods' fault!), Woods produced one of the best-made tents I have ever seen. Made out of bullet-proof nylon to prevent small ice blocks from falling through the fabric, it was supported by an aluminum frame and adjustable legs made by Alcan Aluminium Ltd. so that it could, if necessary, be erected on a steep slope without cutting a ledge. Four hoop poles were slotted into the frame to support the material, along with other poles threaded laterally through the material. The fabric could be tensioned around the aluminum frame to keep it rigid, and had entrance doors at both ends. Nylon reinforcing tapes were sewn into the material, from which guy lines (normally climbing ropes) could be secured. A frost liner was installed inside the tent, and plywood panels were also provided, in case a floor was necessary. Provision was made for stoves to be hung from the tent to prevent them being kicked over.

An insulated Weatherport hut was purchased from the 1981 American Medical Research Everest Expedition for use at advance Base Camp. It broke down into seven porter loads for carrying, and made a very warm and comfortable communal tent for cooking, eating, and talking. Other personal tents were also used at Base Camp to give a higher degree of individual privacy.

Eva foam mattresses were donated by Republic Packaging Ltd. to insulate the floors of the tents, and Therm-A-Rest mattresses were also provided by Cascade Designs Inc. for extra comfort and insulation.

Cooking Equipment

The Sherpas have traditionally preferred to use wood fires for cooking at Base Camp on expeditions. Because of the huge number of expeditions now taking place annually in Nepal, this practice has been having devastating effects on the forests of the mountainous regions of Nepal, and has now been banned. Consequently, we now have to use other fuels. The usual fuel used is kerosene, but this has the drawback of being smelly and messy, and local supplies can be contaminated. Even so, Optimus stoves donated by L.F. Burgess and Associates were used, mainly as back-up stoves at Base Camp. Most cooking, heating, and lighting was done by propane fuel, using equipment donated by B. D. Wait Co. Ltd. and propane cylinders donated by Western Rock Bit Co. Ltd. Large double- and triple-burner Jiffi Ranges were used for the big cooking tents at Base Camp and advanced Base Camp. For the other camps, a hanging stove was designed. It used a regulator from a Primus butane stove (for finer control at low flows) and other parts kindly made by B. D. Wait, with sufficient parts cannibalized from a Bluet stove to allow the French 5200 butane/propane cartridges to be used. Heat loss was minimized by placing the cooking pan inside a larger pan which was in fact a heat shield, with the burner head situated inside the bottom surface. The larger pan was punctured with several holes to encourage air ingestion for combustion, and three chains were attached to its sides to form the hanging arrangement. A copper band encircled the gas cartridge, with an arm extending up into the burner to provide pre-heating of the gas, and an insulating jacket was wrapped around the cartridge. This design allowed for more efficient use of the fuel, and worked very well. B. D. Wait also donated excellent Primus lanterns for illumination in the Base Camp tents, as well as propane heaters for use in the Base Camp tent as the weather got colder. The Canadian Coleman Co. donated folding ovens for use at Base Camp, which gave us the luxury of homemade bread, pies and cakes. They also donated kerosene lanterns.

Oxygen Equipment

The masks, hoses, regulators, and pressure gauges were purchased directly from the 1981 American Medical Research Everest Expedition, supposedly after reconditioning. Two types of masks were used, a simple constant-flow system, which was reliable but inefficient and was supposed to be for Sherpa use, and a sophisticated diluter-demand system, which had a separate delicate valve built into the silicon face mask that only opened when breathing in and then closed upon exhaling. This, in theory, was more efficient because oxygen was not lost during the exhaling part of the breathing cycle. In practice, the valve froze shut on every mask, and rendered them all useless. Invariably, the climber was unaware that the valve was inoperative, and that the only air he was receiving was ambient air sucked through the inlet parts and the mixing chamber of the mask, and credited his poor performance to the effects of high altitude, meanwhile carrying 21 pounds of useless junk up the mountain. Only by monitoring the pressure gauge over a period of time was it possible to ascertain for certain that the system wasn't working.

The oxygen cylinders were supplied by Life Support Engineering Ltd. and were another disappointment. Apart from being heavy —13 pounds empty and 17 pounds full—they had not been tightened properly after being filled with oxygen, and at Base Camp about half of them were found to be leaking.

APPENDIX III

SPONSORSHIP and COMMUNICATIONS

John Amatt

Few who listened to the exciting news that a Canadian had stood on the summit of Everest on October 5, 1982 understood the incredible team effort that had produced the achievement and that brought the "instant" news back to Canada. The "team" went far beyond the expedition climbers and support members and the "effort" spanned seven years, three continents, and the investment of several million dollars.

During the early organization of the climb in 1979, it became obvious that, if we were to be successful in financing this venture, the expedition urgently needed the support of a major corporate sponsor, who would not only contribute a large portion of the required funds but who would also lend the expedition credibility in the corporate and consumer marketplace. The announcement by Air Canada in March 1981 that it would sponsor the expedition relieved us of a large part of our fund-raising concerns, but it also placed on us an additional responsibility to respond to the promotional expectations of the airline.

Air Canada had two major themes that they wished to communicate to the Canadian public, both of which would require a high profile by the airline and by the expedition. Earlier research had indicated that Canadians did not hold their national air carrier in high esteem and that there were widespread misconceptions about the operations of this independent crown corporation. By drawing a close analogy between the expedition and itself, the airline hoped to sharpen this somewhat fuzzy image, and build new public awareness of a corporation that was innovative, well-managed, and aggressive in responding to the challenges of the 1980s.

The basic management philosophy of Air Canada held that the principles of professionalism, teamwork, integrity, candor, equality, and adaptability were all integral to running a major national corporation—and, coincidentally, to running an expe-dition to climb the world's highest mountain. By building a high profile for the climb, through carefully positioned advertising and promotions, Air Canada planned to reinforce this message in the minds of the Canadian public. However, equally important in reaching the decision to support the expedition was the fact that the airline had recently received permission to expand its operations into the Indian sub-continent. The expedition would help to create exposure for Air Canada in that part of the world.

With this responsibility created by the promotional objectives of the expedition's sponsor, coupled with the awareness that one of the expedition's key goals was to raise the public profile of mountaineering as a sport in Canada, it was logical that we would eventually gravitate towards television as the medium that would bring our unfolding story back home. But that simple decision did not prove as simple to carry out, since nobody had ever televised an attempt to climb Everest from Nepal. In fact, not only had this never been tried before, but further, there were neither television facilities in Nepal nor satellite transmission stations to send the video signals back to Canada. If we were to proceed with this objective, state-of-the-art technology would have to be used and the entire video editing and satellite transmission facilities would need to be created in Canada, shipped halfway around the earth, and constructed in Kathmandu on a temporary basis for the three-month duration of our climb.

In September 1981, following representations from Mike Breckon of Air Canada, Teleglobe Canada agreed to support the project by providing the satellite transmission facilities. As a federal crown corporation, like the sponsoring airline, Teleglobe saw in the Everest challenge a unique opportunity to show Canada an example of what they did every day of the year: overseas telephone, Telex, and telegraph service, and radio and television transmission facilities to Canadians, through a worldwide network of submarine cables and communications satellite circuits.

Over the months that followed, Teleglobe and its project manager, Terry Brukewich, initiated negotiations with the various Nepalese government departments for permission to install and operate a portable satellite earth station in Kathmandu, and with British Telecom in the United Kingdom and Intelsat in Washington (the international regulatory body for satellite communications), for permission to operate a satellite network between Nepal and Canada. Much to everyone's delight and surprise, since the Nepalese are known to be very conservative about controlling news flow from their own country, agreement in principle was granted in January 1982, although formal permission was not received until the following July, three days *after* the expedition had left Canada for Nepal!

We knew that it was not possible to communicate directly between Canada and Nepal and that any communication between the two countries would need a transit point to link the Indian and Atlantic regions. The network that Teleglobe was required to develop, therefore, was a "triple-hop" satellite system, which would relay the signal to a satellite and back to earth three times as it travelled around the globe. From a temporary earth station in Kathmandu, the signal would travel to a satellite in geostationary orbit 25,000 miles over the Indian Ocean, be bounced back to a ground station in Madley, England, and be relayed to another satellite over the Atlantic Ocean before being returned to Teleglobe Canada's earth station in Mill Village, Nova Scotia. From there, it would be fed to the broadcasters in Canada via a third satellite, the Canadian domestic satellite ANIK-B. It was a space-age system that would later make it possible for Canadians to watch live reports from Kathmandu, an incredible one second after they had been transmitted from Nepal.

The broadcast plan that was developed required the climbers to record their climb of Everest using sophisticated lightweight video cameras and ¼-inch video cassette recorders. These tapes would then be sent down the mountain and carried back to Kathmandu by Nepalese runners, a 150-mile journey that would require several days to complete. Here they would be edited into television programs in the expedition's communications centre in the Everest Sheraton Hotel. (Sheraton Hotels Worldwide were the official hosts of the expedition.) In the communications centre, the Teleglobe technical crew of Doug Titus, Mike Shot, Dick Cushing, Mike Seeley, and Ted Kubow would construct a compact 3.7–metre dish antenna to transmit a high frequency 14/11 GHz (gigaHertz) signal that would be converted by the INTELSAT V satellite over the Indian Ocean to the lower 6/4 GHz band, enabling it to be received by the earth station link in the United Kingdom. This technique, known as cross-strapping, would be used commercially for the first time and would be one of the many world broadcasting "firsts" for which this expedition will be remembered.

To build the complex television and radio production facilities in the Everest Sheraton Hotel, which generously agreed to turn over its entire seventh-floor penthouse to the operation, Nevil Pike of Can-EverEx (the official business agent to the expedition) contracted the Toronto-based Advertel Productions Limited, the first independent videotape production house to be established in Canada back in 1960. In addition, negotiations were initiated with an electronics giant, Hitachi Denshi Limited (Canada), who agreed to lend many hundreds of thousands of dollars worth of sophisticated transmitting, relay, and video equipment to record the event.

Finally, negotiations were concluded with the Canadian Broadcasting Corporation (CBC), who acquired the exclusive Canadian copyright use of the broadcast signals from Mount Everest for their network programs, CBC Sportsweekend, CBC Weekend News, CBC National, CBC Journal and CBC Regional News. In addition, CBC agreed to carry non-exclusive English radio reports, whose rights they shared with a network of private stations that was assembled across the country. French-language radio reports were assigned to the Telemedia network through the facilities of CKAC in Montreal.

In the United States, the ABC television network agreed to carry live televised reports of the expedition on its late news show, ABC Nightline, subsequently making telecommunications history when it sent back the first live television pictures of Mount Everest to 20 million North American viewers on October 1, 1982, just days before the successful summit assault. What made this accomplishment so remarkable was the fact that the signal had to be relayed along a network of five specially constructed microwave links, each composed of receiving and transmitting dishes, across 150 miles of remote and rugged mountainous terrain, before it could be beamed back to North America from Kathmandu using Teleglobe Canada's satellite chain.

Subsequent live aerial views of Everest were also relayed back on the CBC network during the incredible summit fly-bys of pilot Emil Wick, flying a Royal Nepalese Pilatus Porter airplane, whose operational ceiling was supposed to be some 10,000 feet lower than the summit of Everest! Just as impressive as this flying feat, however, was the work of the cameraman, Harry Carson, who braved sub-zero temperatures to video film Everest's summit ridge through the open door of the plane while breathing through an oxygen mask at 30,000 feet! And this was achieved not once but twice, as the summit attempts were taking place on October 5 and 7.

The coverage that resulted from all of this effort was treated with some public disdain by people who had no perception of the Herculean effort put out by a group of dedicated people in Kathmandu and Canada, committed to telling the remarkable story behind a remarkable climb. And while this coverage did not meet all expectations, due to

circumstances that were often well beyond human control, it did serve to create almost 100 percent public awareness of the heroic efforts of a brave group of Canadians.

Future years will no doubt see a "live" transmission from the summit of Everest. When that does occur, it would be wise to look back and consider that Canada was first in bringing its technology to bear on this challenging problem.

APPENDIX IV

PHOTOGRAPHY
Pat Morrow

The photographic documentation of our expedition can be cleanly divided into two categories: the foothills approach, and the climb itself. Our obligation as an expedition of snapshooters was to provide images for our principal corporate sponsor, Air Canada; our equipment and food suppliers; purchased newspaper and magazine rights; General Publishing Co. Ltd., the publishers of this book; Programmed Communications Limited, who would produce a variety of audio-visual shows for our public lecture program; and a variety of others who would later produce material commemorating our success. The latter included a feature story in *Equinox* magazine, a CBC television special and a National Film Board travelling photography exhibit.

With this sense of obligation hanging over us, I undertook to encourage everyone on the team not only to wear a camera but to use it even under extremely adverse conditions. As a result, it is probable

that ours has become one of the better documented expeditions in the history of Everest exploration, with over 26,000 photographs taken during the three-month climb.

When we left Kathmandu, the country was wrapped in the gloom of its summer monsoon, a time of soul- and equipment-destroying downpours. The morning almost without exception dawned clear, with a rosy glow on the eastern aspect of the peaks. Strong, undiluted light would provide striking backlit scenes: steam rising from yak backs; vapour escaping through thatch and slate-roofed huts; brilliant spectral highlights glinting off the countless rice paddies. As the midday sun dissolved into a heavy mist, to be followed closely by a deluge, an occasional light ray would sneak through, brightening the colours of a village, or spotlighting an individual cottage.

We relied on Kodachrome 64 almost exclusively to handle this wide range of conditions, with some Ektachrome 400 used inside teahouses and at dusk. Most teahouses have such dark interiors that a flash was needed even with 400 ASA film. This helped add life to facial features and clothing colours when used on dull days, usually at 1/16 or 1/8 power.

Although Leica was selected as the official camera of the expedition, the individual choice of cameras was left up to us by Wild Leitz Canada Limited. Consequently, a variety of models was used, based on our previous mountain experiences. Generally, the automated cameras performed well in the uniform light of the trek, making candid photography considerably easier. However, the same cameras when used in auto mode in the snowy mountains almost always yielded underexposed images. The lassitude instilled by altitude undid any attempts to manually override the equipment in such conditions.

The most satisfactory way of carrying the camera gear was in a Lowe frontal hip pouch, which can be reached into without setting one's pack down. It ensures a certain degree of waterproofing as well. Another useful bag was the Tamrac Chest Pouch, which some preferred. A Chinese-made umbrella (available in Kathmandu) provided excellent protection when shooting in mist and light rain, while the Nepalese version merely slowed the velocity of the rain drops.

A sturdy tripod, such as the Leitz Tiltall, is a must for dawn and dusk situations with 'tele' lenses. Who carries all of this gear? If you can hire a porter to carry most of your personal effects, it will facilitate picture-taking opportunities. Make sure the porter understands he is to remain close behind (not ahead, because if you stop he will continue indefinitely), in case you need to draw upon the supplies in his pack.

In the hip pouch, a medium wide-angle lens such as a 28 mm, a 35–70 mm zoom, and 80–200 mm zoom offer an excellent range while keeping the weight down. On your back you could carry a day pack with water bottle, sweater, sun cream, etc., a few extra rolls of film, and a compact flash unit.

Because this is a popular trekking route, the local people, particularly the women, are reluctant to be photographed. Naturally, if you are staying with a group or family for any length of time, the picture-taking opportunities increase. If you

are passing through and see a chance for a portrait, it is best to go through your guide/porter in making a request, particularly in someone's home, being careful not to offend by violating some unknown protocol.

On the other hand, fine candid portraits are possible without invading anyone's privacy in the Saturday market in Namche Bazaar, or on any day in Kathmandu, where you can get good close-ups unobtrusively by lurking in the shadows with a 100 to 200 mm lens.

Some photographers will do anything to break the ice—I unwittingly provided some comic relief (mostly for myself) when squatting to photograph a classroom of young monks reciting prayers. The crotch of my pants blew out from knee to knee. My photo shows a row of averted eyes.

Once on the mountain, where we experienced instant winter conditions, weight and simplicity became of tantamount importance. To maintain shutter and meter function, we wore cameras inside parkas, producing them only when taking a photo. Prolonged exposure to cold temperatures would first affect the meter and then the shutter. The camera was kept in the tent overnight and in some cases nestled in the sleeping bag, an unwelcome bed partner.

Spare bodies and lenses were carried only as far as Camp II, since weight above this point became more and more a critical factor. My own preference tended towards the wider angle lenses, because of the immensity of the ice formations in the icefall and the immediacy of the huge faces in the Western Cwm. A 20 mm and 28 mm were used most, with the medium and 'tele' zooms

coming into play for portraits of the climbers and the surrounding peaks.

On the mountain, Kodachrome 25 came to the fore, with its neutral snow tones. Bright snow and high intensity UV rays gave exposures 2¼ stops less than those used on the trek in. Exposure measurements were read from your own mitts, or by moving in close to other climbers, because a direct reading from the snow would stymie the meter. On summit day I was forced to wear the camera outside my suit, and water dripping from the oxygen mask froze into a 1-inch-thick lump of ice on top of the camera housing. The meter died early that day, but since lighting conditions were similar to those encountered during the previous six weeks, I managed to rely on memory, bracketing slightly to ensure proper exposure.

Although I had polarizing filters along, I rarely used them because of the danger of underexposing the sky and having dark forms in the foreground, such as tents or rocks, bleed into the sky. The skylight filter provided lens protection and warmed the shadows slightly.

I tried lithium meter cells, which are supposedly good for cold conditions and longevity, but I have had better luck since with the standard silver oxide variety.

Due to their non-restrictive properties, I preferred mitts to gloves while shooting. I had to be careful that sleeve cuffs and mitten ends did not get into the corners of my photos.

The Leitz Tiltall tripod was used around Base Camp for 'tele' views of the Khumbu glacier, and moon-bathed only scenes. A lightweight, two-foot-high tripod was carried as far as Camp II. I found a "C" clamp ice ax attachment not as effective because when the ax is driven into snow for stability it held the camera too close to the ground to be of any use.

The greatest threat to the spontaneity of the climb was the obtrusiveness of the photographer. I had to work hard to avoid merely annoying my climbing partners and, more seriously, interfering with their progress (and possibly endangering them and myself). I often had to preplan picture-taking sessions, and steam ahead of a group in order to set up a shot, or at least have my camera handy (not in pack) for the action shots.

VIDEO

To record the climb for television, we used Hitachi VK C1000 cameras and Futrek FX2V ¼-inch video cassette recorders. Although at the forefront of current technology, these units, together with a couple of spare batteries, weigh in at a hefty 12 pounds.

The camera functioned admirably in cold, but the batteries and the VCR unit suffered from the cold and rough handling. The eyepiece on the camera was particularly vulnerable, eventually tearing off completely from being taken in and out of the pack. The zero balance setting was the only manual control we had to monitor, since exposure was automatic and very accurate. To simplify the system, we modified the camera to activate it by switching on the VCR, but this distracted from the picture taking at times. Also, when the unit was turned off at the end of a picture-taking sequence, the recorder would rewind the last

10 seconds of the tape, erasing that portion. Often we would forget to overshoot to compensate for this, and lost some critical footage.

The cameras came with a limited medium-length zoom lens. A wide angle lens would have eliminated a lot of panning.

Our biggest problem was that the Nickel cadmium batteries were good for only about five minutes of filming in cold weather. A technician later ascertained that these batteries had picked up moisture on the trek in and were operating at less than their estimated 40 minute life. He also suggested that lithium cells may have been a better choice, eliminating the need for the solar panels that we carried as far as Camp II to recharge the nicads. If we had had a voltage meter along it would have eliminated some guesswork in selecting batteries for the day's shooting.

The built-in microphone in the camera provided excellent sound-on capabilities, which even picked up the photographer's own heavy breathing.

The ¼ inch cassette tape gave 20 minutes of footage, with no jamming problems encountered.

Focus was fairly difficult, even discounting the problem of frosted goggles. We ended up using estimated distance settings most of the time, which was satisfactory.

The solid state construction of the camera allowed you to include the sun directly in the picture with no fear of the internal mechanisms self destructing.

Due to its weight and vulnerability, at least at this early stage of its development, we found that the video recorder was not completely suited to coverage of a climb in such

rigorous conditions. The unit finally froze solid at the South Col. Had I been using a compact 16 mm or Super 8 camera, I could have protected it with the warmth of my clothing, and we would have had footage all the way to the summit.